M000203525

how to *date* your spouse

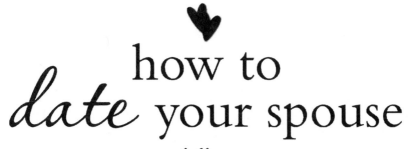

how to
date your spouse

A Couple's Guide to *falling* and *staying* in Love

Lindsey K. Rietzsch

spring creek
BOOK COMPANY
Provo, Utah

© 2008 Lindsey K. Rietzsch
All Rights Reserved

ISBN: 978-1-932898-88-0
e. 1

Published by:
Spring Creek Book Company
P.O. Box 50355
Provo, Utah 84605-0355

www.springcreekbooks.com

Cover design © Spring Creek Book Company

Printed in the United States of America
10 9 8 7 6 5 4 3 2 1
Printed on acid-free paper

Library of Congress Control Number: 2008924218

ACKNOWLEDGMENTS

Marriage is the most sacred union in which much respect is given in society to those who treat it as such. I would like to acknowledge and thank all of those who have been a blessed example of a healthy marriage or a positive influence in my life.

This book is dedicated to my husband and son. Both of you have been my inspiration for writing this book. Without you, my dreams would have seemed impossible to reach. Thank you for making each day a little bit of heaven on earth and keeping me focused on what's really important.

I want to thank my family for acknowledging my talents as a child and encouraging me to nurture them for the benefit of others. Thank you for always believing in me and celebrating my successes with me as well as supporting me during my failures.

A special thanks to my community and to all of those who have inspired me in one way or another to pursue this special project. It is my hope that the message this book offers will inspire and influence couples all around the world to strive at putting their relationships with their spouses and families first.

TABLE OF CONTENTS

Chapter 12 — Page 59

congratulations!

Take what you have learned and put it to use. There are many rewards and benefits in doing so. Learn to find your motivation and go for it!

Chapter 13 — Page 61

50+ best dates ever!

Don't have time to brainstorm creative date ideas? No problem. It has already been done for you. With 50+ categorized date ideas and details, there's a great date waiting for everyone!

Date Categories:

INTRODUCTION

It is said that in the United States, 50 percent of marriages end in divorce. According to the National Vital Statistics Reports from 2006, figures show that the U.S averages at close to 40 percent for marriages ending in divorce—with most states averaging in the mid to upper 40 percent.

With that number on the rise, it's difficult to not wonder what more can be done to save marriages and relationships. An injured relationship has many similarities to a severe illness. The difference is that you don't see anyone promoting charity events to earn money for research on how to heal relationships. In a society where injured relationships seem to be just as common as cancer and heart disease (the effects sometimes just as devastating), it's no wonder that most HMOs don't cover marriage counseling.

The inspiration for this book began in the spring of 2006 when I was asked to speak at a community function on the topic "How to Date Your Spouse." I was flattered that I had been selected to speak on a topic as exciting as this, yet at the same time nervous as I realized after my presentation all eyes would be on me and my husband for weeks to follow. Despite the risk I accepted the opportunity and in doing so it changed my life in ways I couldn't have imagined.

During my preparation I became very passionate about the subject. Ideas seemed to spring up left and right as I took from my own experiences and the experiences of other successful couples. I recall intensely searching for ideas and information, only to discover that most of the current written literature that existed on this topic was far more focused on the professional/sociological perspective and "what not to do's" rather than the "what to do's" and how to make it fun! Needless to say this is a serious subject that need not be taken with such a serious approach.

I was told by a woman who attended my presentation that if a book ever were to be published on the information I had covered that day, it would be a bestseller! At that moment the light bulb came on. Why not share with the rest of the world the information I had discovered? It was then I was inspired to try something different. I wanted to offer a fun and creative alternative for a problem that seems to have no connection to the word "fun." After all, shouldn't meaningful relationships be fun? It seems that in this day and age most marriages have been milked dry of any fun and excitement. It's time to help bring that excitement back!

I decided to continue studying this topic and adding to what I had already begun. As a result I created an exuberant mixture of relationship "how to's", motivational advice, and new ideas, along with a splash of much-needed humor.

The purpose of this book is not to focus on the grim statistics of marriages and relationships, but instead to offer hope and excitement as a way to recharge what you have already created. This book is written for spouses; however, it can be applied to any type of relationship where love and bonding is desired. If there is a chance for a spark in your relationship, there is hope that this book will ignite that spark into a flame.

The ideas and advice offered in this book can perform wonders on any relationship, but they should not be used in place of a marriage counselor or to solve severe relationship problems for which professional help is required. The concept of this book is unique, as it takes a creative approach to spicing up your relationship and getting the most out of your marriage! It's meant to have fun with and enjoy, and it's meant to evoke new habits. This book is one of the best investments you could ever make for yourself, besides owning stock in Microsoft.

Be careful—as friends and family become intrigued by your newfound happiness and excitement, they are going to be drawn to spending more time with you. This book will open more doors than just within the realms of your marriage. With that said, it's time to sit back, relax and prepare to be enriched with a new approach to relationship enhancement. Dating your spouse has just become a new pursuit. Let the fun begin!

CHAPTER 1

the myth

Believe it or not there is a universal myth that has been circulating around the globe for many years. This myth often creates a sense of fear among those who have yet to tie the knot. To singles everywhere it is being suggested that to be married is to be doomed to a life of slaving over children and keeping up with the Joneses.

Truly, once you have found your "other half" and have made that commitment to be there in sickness and in health, you've just signed a contract without reading the fine print—"no refunds or exchanges after 30 days."

Let's face it, after that newlywed stage your 30 days is up! You then realize that most everything there is to know about your spouse you have already learned. Finally you have reached that level of stability commonly referred to as "routine." Once there, you're too comfortable to break away. That's when going out with your spouse consists of the usual dinner and a movie. You visit the same old places and order the usual. In fact, the waitresses know you by name, how you like your steak cooked, and they always remember to leave off the onions.

The only topic keeping your conversation alive over dinner is what your kids did or didn't do today. By the time that subject is dried out, the movie is about to start, thank goodness, because the two of you are no longer obligated to verbally interact. Yes, you both can now lean back in your cushioned seats and let your thoughts be dominated for the next two hours. Hey, why not even get a little bit of shuteye? It's been a long day and the dark air-conditioned theater is calling out to your weary minds and bodies.

If you are nodding your head right about now, then you too have fallen into this timeless trap. Here's the million-dollar question everyone is dying to know: "Does marriage have to end up this way?" My answer to that is, "Absolutely not!" Realize that as soon as Friday night feels no different than Monday night, it's time for some spice!

Before you can apply this book to your relationship it's important to understand which type of couple you and your spouse are. There are commonly three types of couples that quickly lose the spice in their relationships. They are:

Mundane and Married (M&M)

If you fall into this category, you have come to accept that the only benefit of being married for as long as you have is that now you are finally set in your ways. Comfort has played a big role in your daily routine. You can't remember the last time you planned a vacation or went out of town. All you know as that you aren't planning anything soon. Why leave your 25-mile radius when everything you really need is within three blocks of your house?

Friends are a rarity these days unless they are willing to conform to your current lifestyle. Attending social events means stepping out of your bubble and change is something your marriage doesn't welcome. Saying "No" to weekend plans eliminates any unwanted stress and anxiety. Searching for parking spots and sitting in crowded restaurants sounds just as appealing as sunbathing in Antarctica.

Trapped by Time (T.T.)

On your 10-year anniversary the fact that your spouse even remembered it was the highlight of the evening. With all of the events that occupy your calendar it's amazing when time is ever found for casual conversations. Sipping lemonade on the front porch is just a memory these days.

Time has you wrapped around its finger. You both are slaves to the demands of your lives. Your friends and family are so used to you and your spouse's busy and hectic schedule that they rarely call and invite you to dinner. Being able to spend one evening alone with your spouse seems less likely than finding beef tenderloin on a vegetarian's shopping list.

Budgeting Yet Broke (B.B.)

You were hopeful in the beginning that by sticking to a strict budget the two of you would be able to save up for a fun trip or new set of furniture. Two years later the only benefit of your tight budget is the security of knowing that your power will be on next month.

It would be a real delicacy to be able to purchase fast food. "Burgers to go" only occurs on special occasions. Renting movies on the weekend means that the phone payment will be $10 short. An evening of fun with your significant other consists of bottled water and people-watching in the park.

There are many other circumstances that seem to hold back couples from the pleasures of dating. In reality, quality time is always more important than quantity time. It's not how often we are able to get away, or how much money we have to put into a fun evening. This is a common mistake that many couples make. Rather, it's about how willing we are to get creative and develop an atmosphere that evokes good quality time and cultivates romance back into our relationships.

Being able to communicate your feelings and needs in a

comfortable environment will bless your marriage immensely. Dating your spouse should evoke opportunities to do so. On the subject of connecting with your spouse, Nancy and Jim Landrum, authors of *How To Stay Married & Love It!* point out:

> *"Emotional intimacy—the sense of being connected, the heart of a SoulMate relationship—is created and maintained only by communication of your feelings and needs. Intimate SoulMate love is never found in, or sustained by, communication that is limited to cliché, fact, or opinion."*

As husband and wife you have the responsibility, obligation and opportunity to develop better communication in your relationship. Marriage can and should be the greatest thing that happens to you in this life, along with having children. We need to make the most of it and work to make it that great experience we dreamed about when we were young. Ignore all of the myths that you've heard. No more focusing on what you can't do—start focusing on what you can do.

Dating your spouse doesn't have to be boring, stressful or even expensive! Throughout the next chapters I will shed some light on new subjects that most couples have completely missed in their marriages. Prepare your mind to be enlightened and to be opened to new ideas and objectives that will change how you date your spouse!

CHAPTER 2

date your spouse?

So, why is dating so important after the fact that you've already won your sweetheart over in marriage? Shouldn't those dating days be over now? Married couples should focus on more important things such as finances, children, and family goals, right?

I couldn't disagree more.

William F. Harley Jr., the author of *His Needs Her Needs for Parents*, says:

> *"Before you were married, you probably planned your dates around recreational activities. You wanted to be certain that you were both enjoying yourselves when you were together, so you chose activities that would make that possible. You may not have known it at the time but if you hadn't spent your recreational time with each other, you probably wouldn't have created the romantic relationship that led to marriage."*

Harley further goes on to say that it is crucial to do the recreational activities you enjoy most with your spouse. If you're spending your most enjoyable time apart from each other, you're not in a romantic relationship. If you have your "movie friends" and your spouse has his "golf and skiing buddies" it's very likely that you are spending more and more time away from each other. This is dangerous. If you love to ski and you are doing it with other people, you will bond with those people. Shouldn't you be bonding with your spouse?

Spending precious bonding time with others steers you onto the dangerous road that often leads to an affair. Connecting with someone of the opposite sex begins an emotional affair which often leads to a physical affair. Sure, your husband may be with his male buddies when he's out on the weekends and there may not be an affair to worry about. But for every day he spends with someone else, whether male or female, that's a day that your love bank receives zero deposits. Troubled marriages often have these division lines that create jealousy and loneliness.

Many wives have a "best friend" as do husbands. Realize that as husband and wife you should consider each other best friends. If you find it difficult to visualize hanging out with your spouse, talking about goals, and enjoying your favorite pastimes together, you have a problem. If you'd rather call your best girlfriend or buddy than your spouse when you have exciting news, when you want to buy tickets to a show, or go to that new store that just opened down the street, you have a problem. Always put your spouse first! Make going to that show a date with your spouse. Our families will always be our families, our friends will always be our friends, but if we neglect spending time with our spouse we may not always have one.

Let's take a quick travel back in time to a day when the two of you were single. Remember all the things you did to impress each other? The body language, the flowers, and the flirtatious laughter—you were actually concerned about what you wore and how you looked. In fact, you had to get approval from your roommates, even from your little sister, before you dared to leave the house. Your car was always clean and your breath smelled like a peppermint air freshener. Your mind raced with thoughts about how the evening would go, what he/she would think about you, and what you would end up talking about. You wanted to say all the right things so you didn't mess it up for yourself. If it was you that had planned the dates you'll remember that the evenings were actually "planned." Whether you made reservations, bought movie tickets or prepared a home-cooked dinner, you put time and thought into the preparation.

You might say to yourself, "Well, now the dating days are over. There's not enough time or money to do all things we used to enjoy. We're different people now and have more responsibilities." Well, you couldn't be more wrong. The dating days are never over. But we may have to re-evaluate the definition of the word "date."

According to Webster's Dictionary, the definition of a date is simply "an appointment." To date or to court someone is defined as "to seek the favor of, to gain the affections of; to seek in marriage, to woo, to play the lover." If we combine the two definitions we have, "An appointment to gain the affections of ..." How interesting! Think about that for a minute.

So, what does it mean to date your spouse? For many, leaving the house and spending money is the first thing that comes to mind. How wrong they are! If you lived in an earlier time period where money was sparse and leaving the house meant walking for miles on dirt roads or through sagebrush just to get to the nearest town, then dating your spouse surely would consist of neither of these components. So, were our ancestors more creative than us or did they just focus all their time and energy on keeping up the farm?

According to Marcia Swell, author of *Pilgrims of Plymouth*, the following depicts the early pilgrim conditions.

"The typical pilgrim home consisted of very little furniture. The husbands were the ones to have a good chair generally, and

the others sat on long benches. For eating, there was a table made of one long board set on two barrels. For plates they used what was called a "trencher" made of wood or pewter. Although they did use spoons, the most useful utensil was their hands."

Meager conditions didn't stop the pilgrims from having fun. Plymouth had to have been a happening place in its time—after all, it had no competition. I can imagine that chopping wood became a contest, rounding up the chickens became a sport, and a BBQ with the neighbors meant having the Indians over for some good food and exchange of gardening tips.

There was square dancing in the moonlight, storytelling by candlelight, singing by the fire, and exploring untamed country. These days the only exploring we do is on the clearance racks at the mall. Storytelling for us means telling the story about the guy that just cut us off in traffic.

To keep the love alive in your marriage you'll need to try new things (that's how we explore) in new places. It will mean experiencing more fun and having healthier conversations. What is a healthy conversation? Anything that promotes positive behavior and attitudes. After all, when we feel good, we are likely to have more fun.

No matter what generation you are from, what your financial circumstances are, or what your cultural differences may be, a good marriage is molded by the interest you display in your spouse. That's what dating really is, right? When you were single weren't you always trying to get to know your date a little better each time? It always feels good to have someone interested in you. That means you are interesting!

Family therapist Virginia Satir brings up an interesting point on this topic. She refers to married couples as "architects of the family" and notes that most children have a difficult time visualizing their parents being physically affectionate towards one another. Many adults express that they find it tough to imagine how their parents ever got together in the first place. As children grow up and have relationships of their own, they often model behaviors they learned from their parents. Thus, if you put your spouse last and rarely display affection toward him or her, the odds are likely that your children will do the same in their relationships. Now, I think you can understand why dating your spouse is serious business!

Dr. Willard F. Harley says,

> "It's incredible how many couples have tried to talk me out of having them spend more time together. They try to convince me that it's impossible, or they argue that it's impractical. But in the end, they usually agree with me that without time for undivided attention, they can't recreate the love they once had."

The advice and ideas offered in this book may take a little more planning and a little extra effort than what you are used to. However, you wouldn't have picked up this book if you weren't interested in learning how to date your spouse.

In a nutshell, dating is more than just what we do with our spouse or where we take them, it's a way to step away from the demands of life and get to know each other a little better. It's a time to have fun, release our stress and worries, talk about our goals and dreams, and most important, grow together.

CHAPTER 3

to be or not to be prepared!

Have you ever been on a date with a person you weren't really attracted to, yet you had so much fun that you'd easily consider and second or even a third date? Have you ever been on a date with a person you were very attracted to but the night was so boring and dull it ruined the way you felt about that person? What about the date with the attractive person who was so fun and outgoing that you really didn't care how cheap and low-key the date was?

The point I am making is that the level of preparation that goes into planning a date will determine its outcome. It doesn't matter how great you look or how good you smell; if you don't put effort into the date you will have a negative outcome. The outcome will determine your feelings about the other person (your spouse). Thus an over-the-top date equals over-the-top feelings and emotions.

The largest factor behind why most couples rarely date is the fact that they don't plan it. It's very easy to get caught up with the demands of life. Trying to plan an evening out at the last minute can seem like too much work. Even though going out sounds like fun, staying home is just easier. Realize that when you plan it, it's going to happen. Be in control of your life; don't let your life control you. Avoid the dangerous trap of:

"What do you want to do?"

"I don't know, honey. What sounds good to you?"

"I don't know, whatever you want. You decide."

This method of date planning will lead to frustration and boredom, which eventually will lead to lack of interest in your spouse. Also, avoid being wishy-washy. When you make plans, keep them! People who change their minds more often than their socks send a message to the world that they are unstable and insecure. How can you grow to love and lean on your spouse when she takes 20 minutes to decide whether or not to order plain lemonade or raspberry lemonade? Knowing what you want well in advance displays confidence, which of course is always very attractive.

Another factor that inhibits marital dating is the old idea that women should never take the lead. If you think it's not ladylike for a woman to take a man out on a date, good luck with your marriage! A relationship is 50/50. If one person is doing all the work and all the planning, he/she is bound to get burned out. Nothing feels better than serving someone you love. In return you feel cared for and loved when you are being served.

So, where do you start in this preparation process, and what about just being spontaneous? Always remember that change is good. If you are always spontaneous then surprise your spouse by actually planning an evening. Planning a date shows that you are thinking about your lover well in advance. She must mean something to you since you went out of your way to make plans. Being spontaneous is great if you are always a planner. It shows your spouse that for once you are letting loose and are open to his ideas, wants, and needs. Be careful, though. Being too spontaneous can also send a message that you do not want to put effort into planning a special or fun evening. Look for a healthy balance.

All right! Let's begin preparation for your new lifestyle.

1. Get a Calendar

The first step in getting started on your new dating adventures is to get yourself a calendar. Make sure your calendar is in clear view where the both of you can always see it. A good place to hang your calendar is the kitchen as it is often a gathering place. Roll the dice to decide who will be the first to plan. Next, decide how often you are able to date. Once a week, twice a month—just remember never to go more than 30 days without having a date. So, if you decide on every other Friday, then you would block out every other Friday on your calendar for the rest of the year.

Be sure to rotate and write who is planning each date so you don't forget. It's okay to be flexible if plans change or events come up. However, you must make the date night a priority. Whenever possible, always put your date nights first. Your time away together and how you spend it is more important than any sale at the mall or neighborhood BBQ. If you have children they will understand that your time together is important. As you make each other a priority, you will send a message to your children that you value your relationship and your marriage. They will learn from your example and in return will develop important values that will benefit their relationships in the future.

2. E for Effort

In grade school the grading system is lettered A, B, C, D, and F. An A means "Awesome" and an F means "Failure." In between you have Barely awesome, just Cutting it, and Don't even bother. So what happened to E? E stands for effort. Realize that the "gray"ding scale is gray while effort is black or white. Either you put forth effort or you don't. There is no such thing as a little effort. In my opinion, that is why E is not found in the grading system.

I think it's a good idea to grade your dates at the end of the night. Never use the grading system as a way to criticize or attack your spouse. Discuss what worked and what didn't. This is important so you and your spouse avoid sour dates in the future. If effort is involved 95 percent of the time, the date will be an A+. Unforeseen circumstances may occur and can alter our attitudes and plans, which can spoil our fun. Just remember you are in control of your attitude. You will not have control over unforeseen events or your spouse's reaction, but you do have control over how you respond, and that can change the outcome.

Get excited about your night to plan! This is your time to impress your spouse. You are playing a big role in the direction that your relationship heads. Take this opportunity seriously. If you had a dull week, plan some fun. If you had a long, hard week, plan some relaxation. Use this to your advantage. The perks and rewards will be worth every penny and minute that you put into your planning. That, of course, is priceless!

3. Budget!

If you are a wife who doesn't work outside the home, never feel that because you are not contributing financially to the household that you cannot take your husband out. If you share an account, budget a certain amount that cannot be exceeded each month for date nights. You can still plan surprises and have independence in your planning.

Husbands, let your wives have their freedom when planning dates. Trust them and encourage them. Never complain if you disagree as to how the money was spent. As long as the agreed amount was not exceeded you should have no complaints. A happy spouse has its benefits!

The outcome of the date has nothing to do with the amount of money you have. Creativity, quality time, effort, and attitude have everything to do with the outcome. If you have little money to work with (a B.B. couple), don't fear. You can actually have some of the most memorable and meaningful dates. Your dates will require more creativity and therefore should be quite original. These often can be some of the best dates you'll ever have. Chapter 13 offers ideas for couples who fall into this category.

If you have the money to spend but have always been very frugal, learn to loosen up when it comes to date nights. Your spouse may feel that he/she is not worth much if you are not willing to spend anything on the date. You don't need to go overboard, but taking your wife to a restaurant and limiting her to ordering from the appetizer menu is no different than heating up TV dinners when a roast is sitting in the fridge. Yes, I'm sure the free chips and salsa are filling, but look at the bigger picture. Look for ways to budget so you can afford a nice dinner. Choose to cut back in other areas such as groceries or personal wants.

It's a great idea to budget for two big date nights per year. Plan ahead for when they will be. These will be the nights you should plan on spending some money. Examples would be a concert, a major event, an out-of-town excursion, a pricey restaurant or an expensive gift. These dates will get you excited and give you something big to look forward to, especially if they will be a surprise.

Each spouse should get one night per year (not counting anniversaries and birthdays) to plan a spectacular date. It is important to avoid anniversaries and birthdays when planning these events because your spouse needs to be spoiled on dates other than the expected ones. Getting special treatment always feels great, especially when you are not expecting it!

4. Play the Role

No, playing the role does not require any acting skills. I can remember when I was in college and how exciting it was to get taken out on a date by someone who barely knew me. He was on his best behavior and I was on mine (most of the time). This meant we'd strive for a near-perfect evening so there would be a possibility for a second date. We both wanted to make a good impression and worked our magic to impress each other.

Now that you're married you can still play the role of "being taken out" or "taking out." Imagine that each date is your first date; this will help you stay focused on impressing each other. If you are the one planning, remember it's always wise to plan a date centered on your spouse's interests. This sends a message that you really care about your spouse and put his/her needs before your own. If you really dislike your spouse's interests, then find a middle ground. Plan a night that complements both of your interests. Either way, the best part about this whole experience is that because you are rotating the planning, both of your needs will be met each month. No more arguing, complaining or feelings hopelessness. Your new dating adventure is bound to please you both!

5. Free Babysitting!

Within your circle of friends and family every married couple faces the moment when there are no babysitters available. Some couples can't even afford a babysitter, let alone trust a teenager or someone else to watch their kids. I have good news for all of you. With everyone being in a similar predicament, why not take advantage of a golden opportunity!

Establish a system in which couples within your circle of friends and family take one night a month in which they watch your children so you can go out. In return you do the same for them. I have known couples who divided up the Fridays in a month. Couple A had the first Friday, Couple B had the second Friday, and so forth. When it rolled around to your Friday, it was your night to babysit. Yes, you would take on all the children of all the couples. The rest of the couples could go out separately or as a group. You may just want to rotate with one other couple who has two children, versus three couples with one child each. However done, this method can work nicely. Babysitting for free one Friday a month really isn't so bad when you look at the benefits. You'll always have a guaranteed babysitter every month at no cost.

CHAPTER 4

get ready, get set!

It is a known fact to most parents that little girls delight in the opportunity to play "dress up." This little girl trait apparently never changes. As little girls grow up they still enjoy dressing up—the only difference is that a credit card is usually involved.

Men may not be as eager to purchase the latest fashions, but most men don't hesitate at the opportunity to flaunt their muscles. In fact, right now all across the globe there are men bench-pressing in gyms, rock climbing outdoors, boxing in basements, and jogging through parks. For most men, getting ready for a date generally consists of the following three components: stomach crunches, washing the car, and applying deodorant. However, no matter what a man's process involves, most want to do all that they can to be appealing to the opposite sex.

Women generally take the getting-ready process a step further. Two hours prior to the doorbell ringing they have already completed a pedicure, applied a face mask, and waxed their legs. By the time the date begins, most women are ready to call it a night from the pure exhaustion of getting ready. Husbands, you now can see why your wives may be a bit disturbed when you fail to compliment their appearance on a daily basis. Women need to be told that they are beautiful as often as possible; we are just wired that way. Wives, it is equally important for you to return the favor!

The longer you have been married the more you may feel that you have lost the passion in dressing to impress. It's possible that the act of "letting yourself go" could be a side effect of mild or severe depression. According to the National Institute of Mental Health, "loss of interest or pleasure in hobbies and activities that were once enjoyed" is a symptom of depression. If this is the case for you, you may want to evaluate the benefits of counseling.

However, many spouses simply become comfortable in their marriage and claim that "dressing to impress" is frivolous behavior. "My spouse loves me for who I am on the inside. Nothing else matters." Sound familiar? I say good for him! Furthermore, wanting to look your best whenever possible is a sign of healthy self-esteem and successful attributes. There should never come a day when we decide to no longer take care of our outward appearance. When this happens a strong message is sent to the world and those around us: "I don't care anymore. I have given up." You have given up on yourself, your goals, and your relationship with your spouse. Rule of thumb—always care.

If getting ready to go out with your spouse does not spark any interest, you may need to adjust your attitude as well as your habits. Let me demonstrate this foreign idea with the classic example of Kirk and Jenna.

Kirk considered himself an average Joe. He owned 10 different shirts (all of which looked alike), but rotated often between his favorite three. He had one pair of jeans that he wore daily and an outdated pair of slacks he hadn't worn since his first job interview. Kirk was perfectly satisfied with his wardrobe and felt that money could be spent on better things.

Jenna, Kirk's wife, had a larger wardrobe than her husband but felt that she no longer fit in her clothes the same way she did prior to having kids. For that reason she also rotated between her five best-fitting outfits. She avoided buying larger clothes as that would mean that she had given up on her quest to lose weight. She hoped and waited for the day that she could fit back into her college jeans. Since having children she could no longer find the time or energy to style her hair. A ponytail was sufficient enough.

Kirk never complained about Jenna's look, although he did start to feel as though their dates were losing excitement. Jenna as well never complained about Kirk. His effort to take a shower and brush his teeth was good enough for her. She did feel that the old connection they used to have no longer existed. However, she figured it was normal after having kids and decided to accept it.

After attending a free relationship seminar one night, Kirk and Jenna agreed to try something new. The concept of "dressing to impress" was more than just a concept, it was a new lifestyle!

"It was so much fun," Jenna said. "I finally caved in and bought something I actually look good in. I've never been a jewelry kind of girl, but I bought some nice earrings and a couple of necklaces. Kirk even bought a new sweater and jeans. It was so good to see him in different colors for once. I went and got a new haircut that was a lot easier to style. We became committed to spending more time on ourselves before we leave the house. It's made a huge difference in our marriage. Kirk loves the new change. It's like we're new people!"

Needless to say, after some minor yet needed adjustments, Kirk and Jenna looked forward to their nights out together. They could not believe they had gone so many years oblivious to this concept!

Wives, when trying to apply this concept within your marriage, Karen Scalf Linamen, author of *Pillow Talk*, suggests the following;

> *"Whenever possible, put your best foot forward. In makeup, hair, dress, fingernails, even a small added effort can reap great*

rewards. It's amazing, for example, what a good haircut can do for the ol' self-esteem. And red toenails, even hidden beneath thick socks and a pair of boots, can make any woman feel sexier.

"Buy silky lingerie. Buckle down and lose those five pounds. Experiment with a new hairstyle or color. Wear bright earrings. Have your nails done. Get contact lenses.

"Call your local department store cosmetics counter and arrange an appointment for a makeover. Most stores offer them free of charge. I recently made an appointment with a cosmetics consultant at Penney's. I happened to like the makeup she used, spent seventy dollars, and walked away feeling like a million bucks. If there's something you can improve about the way you look, why not do it?"

Here are some steps couples can take to make the "getting ready process" something to look forward to rather than dread.

1. Get Ready to Music That Pumps You Up!

Getting ready for your date should be no different than a good workout routine. Find some great music and crank up the volume. When you're listening to music you enjoy, you'll begin to feel good. When you feel good on the inside you'll feel good about what you see on the outside. You'll radiate positive energy throughout the house and you're spouse will appreciate it (if your voice is in tune).

2. Shout Positive Affirmations

As you're having a great time singing and dancing in the shower, begin preparing for your grand entrance. After shutting the water off, throw open the shower curtain, strike a pose and shout, "Yeah, this is what I'm talking about!" Whether you're alone or in the company of your spouse you won't be able to avoid laughter. (Try to remain serious. It will baffle your spouse).

Look for things you like and announce them out loud. "I've lost two pounds!" "I love these shoes!" "Wow, I forgot how great these pants look on me!" "Honey, that color really enhances your eyes!" "I really like the way you smell!" "Tonight is going to be fun!" Never discredit a compliment or you'll soon hear less of them. Thank your spouse and believe him. The more positive you are the better your date will go. You and your spouse will feel great about yourselves. There is nothing more attractive than good self-esteem.

3. Select Your Clothing in Advance

If you have a Friday night date with your wife, you should have decided by Wednesday what you are going to wear. Not only is this wise because you will be prepared (thus save time), but you will also look forward to Friday if you are excited about what you will be wearing. There is nothing more stressful than finding out 20 minutes before your date that the shirt you were planning on wearing to the opera has a juice stain right across the front. After having three months to settle into the fabric, it will take you 24 hours at the least to get your shirt back to normal. Always be prepared!

4. Try Something New!

I've noticed that men and women who never put thought into their wardrobe never look forward to the "getting ready" process. By avoiding this process you set yourself up for just having an okay date. To avoid this, I suggest that you purchase one or two new items for your wardrobe every month. Realize that this does not need to be expensive. It could be as simple as a new necklace, a hat, a pair of socks, $10 lingerie, or sunglasses. It could even be new cologne, scented lotion, lip gloss, or teeth whitener. Anything new that will enhance your appearance is bound to create that confidence and excitement that is so necessary for this process.

It's very possible that you may not even need to buy yourself anything. Husbands will love this! Here's an example: you may own several hats but seldom ever wear them. For your next date choose a hat from your collection (dust it off) and then choose an outfit that goes with it. Most people will choose the outfit first and then come to find that a hat just will not go with it. Try it in reverse. You might even take a pair of earrings and create an outfit from your closet that compliments them. By doing this you will discover new possibilities with your wardrobe and will become just as excited as if you were to buy something new!

5. Give Your Spouse Some Space!

Husbands, give your wife some space! For a change, try getting ready in the basement bathroom. Play your own music and enjoy your own towel! Keep yourself hidden as long as possible. When its time for the date to begin, pull the car out onto the driveway and ring the doorbell to pick up your wife. Greet her with a bouquet of flowers and tell her she looks great!

When you were single, you never saw your date until you rang the doorbell. Remember the suspense?

Overall, take different measures than what you are used to when getting ready to go out. These subtle and fun changes can transform your typical evening into a night you won't forget.

CHAPTER 5
the car ride

A driver's license has been commonly referred to by many as "a ticket to freedom." As we grow older and wiser we quickly realize that the only "ticket" associated with a driver's license is the $80 one we received last month for going 15 miles per hour over the speed limit. Financially we are never free as we continue to pay off the car loan, plus pay for maintenance, registration, insurance fees, and gasoline. We do all this to allow us to safely and legally get from point A to point B. With all the hassle of owning a car, why were we so anxious to pass driver's education? Let me refresh your memory.

Guys, remember pulling up in her driveway in your freshly washed and vacuumed "hotomobile"? We all knew that when there wasn't a dime left in the ashtray and the weather had turned ugly, the best place to spend a date was in that car. Just parking it in front of a spectacular view with the right song playing really got the sparks flying. Right? If you're like the rest of us, of course you spent those times having intelligent conversations about politics, world events, and the stock market. Ah yes, the car was a great refuge from time to time, but the factor it actually played in how the date would end had everything to do with the car ride.

The ride afforded you the opportunity to really get to know your date. You could tell what kind of a person he was by the way he drove, what music was playing, and how dirty or clean the car was. Ladies,if your date actually opened the car door for you, you knew he was a keeper.

The car ride was highly important to how the date started, because whatever conversation took place during the ride to your destination really set the tone for the evening. I remember my dates being so nervous around me that between the long five-minute periods of silence they would ask me a question and then fail to comment after I answered. I also remember guys being so nervous that all they did was talk about themselves. The only way I survived those dreadful nights was to keep telling myself in the back of my mind that enduring the evening meant a free dinner. Sound familiar, ladies? Let me share an example that demonstrates how beneficial the car ride can be.

As a young girl I remember looking forward to long drives out in the country with my dad. With him car rides were never boring. He'd roll down the sunroof on his 1989 maroon Buick LeSabre and allow the fresh country air to whoosh through our hair while singing along to classic rock tunes. The sunlight would glisten on his forehead as he'd tell adventurous stories about his childhood. As I'd gaze out the window into the bright horizon he'd point out landmarks along the way and tell of his connection to them.

Occasionally we'd hit a patch of storm clouds. As the windshield wipers desperately worked to repel the rain from the windshield, my dad would be reminded of a memory that he'd eagerly share. When we'd arrive to our destination I'd always hope for time to fly by so we could return to the car and enjoy another car ride home. Those were the best times that I could always bond and connect with my dad.

Husbands and wives, consider yourselves fortunate to be able to spend time in the car with your spouse. You may be thinking, "Fortunate? Being told how to drive, arguing about the in-laws, and discussing discipline for the kids does not make me feel fortunate."

How right you are! However I'd like to open up a whole new idea about what the car ride should really be about. Willard F. Harley, Jr. notes:

> "If your need for intimate conversation was fulfilled during courtship, you also expect it to be met after marriage. And you will be very frustrated if it is not met. But if it goes on for long, you'll be more than just frustrated—you'll no longer be in love. If you and your spouse are not meeting the need for intimate conversation, your relationship fails the romance test. And it also makes you vulnerable to having an affair with someone who does meet it. Don't let that happen. Apply the friends of good conversation and avoid the enemies whenever you take time to talk to each other."

As I mentioned earlier, what happens during the car ride really sets the precedent for the rest of the evening. This is your chance to really talk and get to know each other. Why talk about all the things that drive you crazy if you really don't have to?

Think about it—no kids, no co-workers, no family, and no distractions. You are alone with your spouse in a locked, air-tight, highly secure facility—your car! This is your moment to talk about all the things that you would never want your parents or kids to hear. Take advantage of this time. Enjoy each other, even if you don't say anything at all! Sometimes silence really is golden.

The car ride can be your ticket to freedom. Roll the windows down; let the wind blow through your hair. Kick off your shoes and turn on your favorite music. Sing and get excited, or relax and unwind. Look at the scenery as you dream about your goals. Look at your spouse as he/she sings to the music and tries to sound good.

Hold hands or put your hand on your spouse's leg. Cherish these moments.

Avoid backseat driving, road rage, criticism, and educating your spouse on traffic laws. If you act like a parent toward your spouse she will in return display "childlike" responses. Should you encounter a traffic jam on your way to dinner, well…that's great! Look at it as an opportunity to have more time to talk with your spouse. Use this precious time wisely. Avoid getting angry at the situation and losing your temper. Also, avoid using this time to bring up negative "baggage" or venting. Talk about your goals and upcoming events.

Here is a fun suggestion I offer to you and your spouse. Put together a collection of all the songs that came out while the two of you were dating. Play these songs during your car ride and they will help you to relive those good memories while reviving those feelings that helped you fall in love. Wear the scents you wore when you first began dating. The combination of the scents and the music will perform indescribable wonders!

Most importantly, use the car ride as a time to get to know one another. The restaurant will have distractions and the babysitter could call at any time with an emergency, so this is the time to compliment your spouse, talk about your dreams and share your happy secrets. If the car ride is used to do these things the date will most likely be a success. A successful date really just means that both of you improved your relationship. The goal that you both will share is to end each date feeling even better about yourselves and your marriage than you did before the date began.

CHAPTER 6
old-fashioned
(the new fashion)

Carmen Ashbury, wife of Alan Ashbury for more than a decade and mother of three boys, said to her husband one April morning, "I haven't been able to help but notice lately how often I see a man walking ahead of his wife in the parking lot, seating himself first at the restaurant while his wife struggles to take off her coat, or sitting in the passenger seat of the warm car while his wife is pumping gas in the cold. What has happened to the 21st century? Gone are the days of opening the door for your wife, having roses delivered just because, dropping your wife off at the entrance so she doesn't have to walk in the snow, or offering to help clean the dishes."

As Alan pondered for a moment on his wife's frustration, a thought came in to his mind. He put down his newspaper, took her hand in his, looked her deep in the eyes and said, "Honey, roses are not enough to describe how I feel about you. Did I ever tell you that whenever you open the door for yourself, the view I enjoy of you is always absolutely breathtaking? When I walk ahead of my sweetheart in a parking lot I am doing so out of protection; any reckless driver would surely hit me first. And I would never drop my wife off at an entrance and make her wait in a lobby all alone. What would that say for me as a husband? As for the dishes…well, I've always been an advocate for paper plates!"

Truly in this day and age more and more couples are lowering their standards and settling for less. It seems as though one morning we all woke up and it was no longer acceptable to have manners. I must have been on vacation the day that Congress passed the law that forbids chivalrous acts. Most of us were in the dark on that one.

On that note I must say to you wives, having the door opened for you is a gesture of respect, not oppression. Would it be acceptable in most countries for a queen to open her own doors and pull out her own chair? Of course she is capable of doing so, but when in the company of others it is a sign of respect.

Husbands, showing the utmost chivalry and respect toward your wife, sends a message to society that you honor, respect, and cherish her. Wives, shame on those of you who refuse to let your husbands do so. Why deny yourselves that honor and respect?

I applaud those husbands who have mastered this area and would never second-guess an act of chivalry. I furthermore propose a challenge to the rest of you who struggle with this concept. As a society, let's all strive to make "old-fashioned" the "new fashion." Husbands, make it clear to your wife that you are on a mission to become her knight in shining armor. In return, wives, do not get out of the car until your husband comes around and opens your door. If he walks ahead, stop in your tracks and wait for him to come back and walk side by side with you. Hold hands.

Wives, slow down when you get near a door and allow your husband to step ahead and open it for you. Not only will it allow him the opportunity to be a gentleman, but you won't have to worry about touching dirty door handles. Most importantly, thank him. Husbands, the more you do this, the more love you will feel toward your wife and her for you. Old habits are hard to break. but if you help each other daily to keep this going it will soon become second nature. It's hard to be mad at each other when you are holding hands, right?

Here are some steps that can be taken to help you implement the "old fashion" gently back into your courtship:

1. Write letters of appreciation

Letters are often the easiest outlet when it comes to expressing feelings. Often the receiver will save them and later read them again during much-needed moments in life. Let your spouse know often how grateful you are to have her in your life. Let her know all the things that you appreciate about her. For best results, give the letters to her right before your dates.

If she is having a bad day, this will soothe her and help her look forward to spending time with you. It's always a nice surprise when they are strategically placed in an area that will surprise her, such as in her purse, on the seat of her car, or taped to the bathroom mirror.

Make sure that your letters are always sincere and genuine. Never use them as a means to create guilt trips, to get your way, or get yourself out of trouble. Susan Page, author of *Now That I Am Married Why Isn't Everything Perfect?* sums this up by saying,

> *"Thriving marriages are characterized by precisely this spirit of generous kindness, including the ability to focus on the positive aspects of your loved one; a feeling of gratitude about your life together; the capacity to accept even the things you don't like so much about your relationship; trust; respect; and the desire to give freely to your partner. These qualities both reflect the goodwill that is already present in your relationship and enable you to generate more of it."*

2. Say "please" and "thank you"

If this comes as a struggle for you, there are deeper problems in your personal life or relationship that you need to take care of. Why is it that it's often easier to be polite to a stranger than it is to those we love?

Not only will these kind words set the tone for your evening, they will also set a fine example for your children and those watching you. Once again, displaying respect for your spouse will perform wonders on your marriage and your relationship. Without realizing it, your spouse will return the favor.

3. Always make the offer

As soon as you learn to forget yourself you'll find that this step is very easy to remember.

Throughout history "offerings" have always been a way of making peace. The term *offering* is defined as "a gift" in Webster's Dictionary. So when you think about offering something to your wife, think of it as "making peace" or giving "a gift." Therefore if you go to the kitchen to get yourself a drink, always ask your spouse if she would like one as well. If you are going to the store, ask her if there is anything she needs. When there is one slice of supreme deluxe pizza left in the box, yes, make the offer. Throughout the course of your date, look for opportunities to make offers. Your wife will notice your kindness and express her appreciation in more ways than one.

4. Ladies first

This applies to buffets, using the restroom, entering doorways, getting in the car, ordering from a menu, and being seated at a table. By allowing your wife to go first, you are putting her needs first and therefore displaying very unselfish behaviors. However, if you roll your eyes, let out a sigh, or complain in any small way, this will counteract your efforts and you may as well have just gone ahead of your wife. If you practice this step like you practice maintaining your employment, you'll be on high ground when the tide rolls in.

5. Express your love often

This is not always easy to do, especially when you feel that your spouse never developed the correct motor skills to be effective at expressing anything. If it's difficult for you to verbalize, write it on a card. Make sure they are your own words; don't just rely on Hallmark®. Realize that if it is difficult for you to verbalize your feelings, doing so will mean more to your spouse than a $1.75 card from the drugstore.

There are many couples who think that by expressing their love often, they are at risk for becoming immune to the powerful effect of those three sacred words. However, love expressions need not always be with words. A hug, a kiss, flowers, gifts, and service are all ways to say "I love you." Remember that enough practice creates a habit!

6. Be aware of her needs

Of course this goes both ways. Never should a spouse (husband or wife) practice selfish behaviors. On the date, husbands, always try to be aware of your wife's needs. If she looks cold, offer your jacket. If she twists her head in order to look around the tall person seated in front of her at the theater, trade seats with her. If she would like "seconds" during a meal, don't remind her about the pounds she promised to lose. Instead, smile and say, "This dinner is delicious!"

When you are concerned about the welfare of your wife and you address them correctly, your wife will feel loved. Wives, you are not off the hook. It is a two-way street these days. If your husband is too tired to stay up with you to finish the sequel to your all-time favorite flick, instead of whining or begging him to finish it, allow him to go to bed. If you put too much garlic in the marinara sauce after knowing how much your husband dislikes it, warn him, but don't be offended if he declines dinner.

7. Learn to accommodate

The Processes of Adaptation in Intimate Relationships Project, known as the PAIR Project, is a research study that was conceived in 1979 at Pennsylvania State University. The project was designed to follow a sample of newlyweds through the first two and a half years of marriage, tracing and gathering detailed information on courtship so that the early years of marriage could be studied in the context of each couple's relationship.

According to the study, accommodation may reflect an adaptation that takes place only after spouses discover, through extensive experience, that their mate is inflexible or unwilling to change. So, it happens you may not be able to change your spouse's mind all of the time, and thus you learn to accommodate.

Let's say you've planned to have dinner on the balcony of your favorite restaurant, mainly for the view. Fifteen minutes prior to your arrival it starts to rain and the balcony is closed. What do you do? Well, you could still enjoy your favorite food and eat inside, or you could eat somewhere that has a covered balcony. If a crisis occurs in the middle of your date, don't panic!

Dates don't always happen as planned. People arrive late, cars get flat tires, and restaurants have waiting lists. Be prepared and keep your cool. It's always smart to have a plan B. Also, if your spouse has planned a date that you're not in the mood for, ask yourself, "Is it really going to hurt me?"

If your safety and well-being are not in jeopardy, learn to bite your tongue, smile and accommodate! If you are able to learn the simple concept of accommodation your spouse will feel stable and secure knowing that you are flexible.

8. Always be interested in the other's welfare

We all have had bad days. Many of us know all too well that it's not always easy to hide our frustration. Not only is it difficult to forget our problems, but it is also hard to pretend they never happened.

If your husband has had one of those days, and you've planned a "romantic" evening on the town, you may just need to prepare yourself to hear about his bad day. It might suck the romance right out of the hotel hot tub, but your husband will know that you care enough to listen and be there for him. Don't get angry and figure that the night has been ruined; allow your spouse to vent and by doing so you will help him adjust his mood.

If you sense your spouse is a little down or isn't feeling well, don't ignore it. Become interested.

9. Make each other top priority

When you are on a date with your spouse it should look to others as though you are enjoying it. Taking and making phone calls, having work on your mind, or rushing to get home on time to see the end of the game or your favorite TV show just will not cut it. You're spouse can sense when he/she is second priority. Twenty years ago dates didn't have the interruptions or distractions of cell phones, Blackberries, pagers, and computers. That could be why relationships lasted longer.

Give your full attention to your spouse. It's probably a good idea to leave the technology at home. Remember, we are trying to be old-fashioned!

10. PDA offers more than words can say!

We all roll our eyes when we see the couple lying on the grass in the park, acting as if they are the only two people that exist in the world! As soon as you hear the words "Get a room!" you know you've entered the zone where mothers passing by are now having to have that awkward conversation with their children about the birds and the bees. I'd like to give you the benefit of the doubt and assume you've never been in this predicament.

Clearly you should respect the unwritten rules of society and keep your intimate moments private. Don't panic; there are still ways that you can publicly display your affection appropriately without being center of the universe! They include holding hands, hugging, walking arm in arm, putting your arm around your spouse or a hand on her knee, and of course a tasteful kiss.

It is very important that you show appropriate public display of affection. Never make your spouse feel uncomfortable or awkward, and at the same time never leave her thinking, "Is my husband ever proud to be seen with me?" Your body language needs to suggest to the world that you love, honor, and respect your spouse. She is the apple of your eye!

Susan Page says that couples who thrive love to talk about how much they love each other and how excited they are to be together. They are affectionate, they have sparkle, they talk effusively about each other and can sometimes be caught acting like newlyweds.

To get the best experience out of dating your spouse, being a little "old-fashioned" will surely get you on that path. These simple gestures will provide your evening with plenty of positive reactions. You'll notice that those watching you will smile and think to themselves, "Now that's how a marriage should be!"

Others around you will even treat you a little better. Without realizing it, you'll create a ripple effect and your old-fashioned ways will rub off onto those around you. Just think about it—your example could not only improve your relationship but revolutionize marriages throughout the world! The way you date your spouse truly has an impact inside and outside of your marriage.

CHAPTER 7

what's the occasion?

I was 18 years old and it was our first time hanging out together. No, it was not a date. My then "future husband" Manuel just needed a ride home that afternoon and later invited me in. Being an exchange student from Germany, he was renting out a room from a host family and thought he'd give me a tour of the house. After meeting the family members, including a goat tied to a fence, I asked if I could see his room. I figured if I could just see his room then that would tell me everything I needed to know about him. Little did I know how wrong I was.

The room was practically bare. There were some soccer bags on the floor and some shirts hanging from the bunk bed. The only other objects my eyes happened to scan were some pencil drawings and textbooks. With not much to judge from I thought, "Maybe this guy doesn't have much going for him. That's strange considering how good-looking he is."

At that moment he walked over to the closet and pulled two boxes out of a bag. He brought them to me and in his foreign accent he said, "Smell these perfumes and tell me which one you like better." Wondering why he had two bottles of women's perfume in his closet, I did what he asked. I looked at the bright and colorful decorated bottles, one blue and green striped and the other orange and red. I took a whiff of each and made my decision. "This one," I told him, holding up the orange bottle. "All right then," he said. "That's my gift to you."

First of all I was amazed because I did not see that coming. Second, he gave me a gift! What woman does not love gifts? I knew at that moment that I meant something more to him than just a ride home. The story doesn't end there. I wore that perfume every day until the bottle ran out. It became my favorite perfume and I was sad to learn that it would not be easy to purchase more. Once I ran out it took us three years to find another bottle since it was made in the Netherlands. Shortly afterwards the company decided to discontinue the perfume. Needless to say, every time I see that cheerful-looking bottle or smell the scent I am reminded of that special moment.

I pose the question to you: "Does there need to be a special occasion in order to give or receive a gift?" Think about that for a minute. Even when we do receive gifts on our birthday they aren't that special to us because we were expecting them. If we receive a gift on a day we weren't expecting one and for no apparent reason, how much more does that gift mean? The best time to give a gift is when there is no occasion.

Being a typical woman, a couple months later I asked Manuel if I could have the other bottle of perfume. I wondered why he hadn't offered me both bottles to begin with. "That's not possible," he said.

"Why not?" I asked.

He let out a sorry laugh and then looked away and said, "I gave it to my ex-girlfriend." And that's where the story ends. Yes, I laugh now, but then it was a different story.

Gift giving is key in a relationship but need not occur that often. In the book *The Five Love Languages,* author Gary Chapman sheds some light on the subject:

> *"I went to Central America and studied the advanced cultures of the Mayans and the Aztecs. I crossed the Pacific and studied the tribal peoples of Melanesia and Polynesia. I studied the Eskimos of the northern tundra and the aboriginal Ainus of Japan. I examined the cultural patterns surrounding love and marriage and found that in every culture I studied, gift giving was a part of the love-marriage process."*

Ask yourself, "When was the last time I gave my spouse a gift?" If you can't remember, then this chapter is for you. Some of the best gifts are not always the expensive, edible, or even the scented kind. They are the thoughtful ones. A homemade card, a home-cooked dinner (especially if you never cook or don't know how) a framed picture of a special memory, a videotape of you expressing your deepest love or reciting a poem, or a trail of notes leading up to a mystery box with a ribbon around it. These are all fine examples of how to express love for your spouse without expressing sorrow for the credit card bill. Just remember my own personal quote: "When it's not about the price, its priceless."

Service — the "other" gift

This one is a favorite to many men and women. When someone sacrifices their time and energy for us, it means more than a bouquet of roses or a steak dinner. Really, money doesn't buy love in the long run. Remember this.

Author Susan Page says couples who thrive tend to be more concerned about whether they are giving their fair share than whether they are getting their fair share. When giving service, choose something that you know your spouse will fall head over heels for. A great example is cleaning! Imagine going out to your car in the morning and noticing that it has been freshly washed and polished. You open the car door and the smell of wild vanilla greets you. Looking down at the floor you notice that the mats have been cleaned and the floor has been vacuumed. Then you notice a small card on your dashboard with a smiley face that reads, "Have a great day!"

After that, you would actually have a great day. Imagine that your spouse cooked a delicious dinner for you and afterward was too tired to clean up. That night after your spouse goes to bed you creep downstairs and take care of mop-up duty. The next morning your spouse wakes up dreading the day, afraid to face the big pile of dishes awaiting in the kitchen. Imagine the shock on his/her face when he/she walks into a spotless kitchen and notices a small card on the counter that reads, "No, this is not a dream. Enjoy your day!"

The secret is to pick something that will mean a lot, whether it's something your spouse never has time to do, or it's something he/she dreads doing. Do it with a positive attitude and without any expectations. Trust me; in return this act will benefit your marriage in more ways than you thought possible.

Gift-giving "don'ts"

Never give gifts in hopes to get something in return. Also never use gifts as a way to make up for a wrong doing. Every time your spouse looks at that gift he/she will be reminded of your wrong doing. Plain and simple, it is just a bad idea. Gifts should not be used as a tool to say sorry, gain favor, or get what you want. Gifts should be given when you really want to express your love for your spouse "just because." Finally, when receiving a gift, never say, "Okay…what did you screw up?" or "What is it you want?"

Your spouse may have given you a gift as a way to honestly express his love. Comments such as these will destroy any future motivation for gift giving. Always give your spouse the benefit of the doubt.

CHAPTER 8

mystery isn't history

Ladies, you have all heard or uttered the common infatuated statement, "He's so mysterious." The batting of the eyelashes, the intoxicating stare and then add a couple of O's to drag out the "so," and you know what I'm talking about. Now in that sultry voice repeat after me, "He's soooo mysterious." Sound familiar?

Women all over the world have said this at one point in relation to someone they were infatuated with. The James Dean, the Brad Pitt, the singer in that high school band, the guy that worked at the car wash, the stranger you sat by on the plane, or the customer who every now and then came into your place of work and gave you that look. Naturally you were determined to figure him out. What was it about him that had you so drawn? Most likely, all of the unanswered questions and details (such as: Where is he from? What kind of music does he like? Is he single? When is his birthday? Does he want to get married? How many children does he want? What are his talents, hobbies, interests, goals?) kept him in your dreams and thoughts.

As women we like to figure people out. We like to analyze, guess, and speculate. When we're left puzzled or without a clue it drives us crazy! We just want to know all the juice all of the time. In those moments when we are uncertain, suspicious, or curious, that is when our minds go wild. For good or for bad we have this drive inside of us to figure "it" out. Whether "it" be a person, a situation, a secret, a feeling, or a plot, we are all over "it." No wonder the quiet, low-key, hence "mysterious" guys were always at the top the top of our list. We wanted to understand them!

It's not that different for men, either. Guys enjoy a challenge. The less they know about a woman the more they want to get to know her. Eventually when they know too much the excitement is gone. This of course depends on the facts they discover about her. It's a common piece of advice that men and women share when they say, "Never reveal too much on the first date." How true this is! You always want to keep the other person interested because once they guess the ending to the story, well . . . they lose interest in reading the book.

So how does this apply in a marriage? If your days are becoming a routine and you never getting time alone, your relationship is crying out for some mystery. How can we be mysterious when we're together just about every day of the week? It's more possible than you may think. Consider what you do in your own personal time. You may go to the gym, go mountain biking, go see a movie with friends, or listen to music.

Anytime you have free time for yourself it can be good to spend it away from the house. Just a few hours a week alone doing something you really enjoy can create some mystery for your spouse. Because your spouse is not with you in your spare time, he/she will be interested in how you spent it.

When being mysterious, remember that secrets are not a good idea unless they are good secrets that you plan to eventually reveal to your spouse, such as a secret date, a surprise party or gift, or exciting news. Instead of secrets, we'll refer to them as surprises. These are a great tool for keeping mystery alive! Your spouse will have fun trying to figure out what you are up to or what you may be planning. Since you are withholding information, you become mysterious. You may encourage your spouse to play detective and require that he/she figure out the secret without your help. Leave some clues around to throw him/her off, but most of all, have fun with it!

There are some important rules you must remember when applying some mystery to your marriage. There is a good mysterious and a bad mysterious. Not being honest, keeping secrets or doing hurtful things is not the mysterious you want to be.

Rule #1

Don't use mystery as a way to make your spouse jealous. Avoid this childish game like the plague.

Rule #2

Never give the silent treatment or frequently disappear to make your spouse wonder where you are. Your spouse will not view your new disappearing act as talent. Instead, these silly childhood games will very quickly destroy your marriage.

Overall, don't be an open book all of the time. You don't need to bombard your spouse with all of the details of your day. At the same time don't take on the character of James Bond. It may sound fun at the time, but too much mystery and surprise can create some uneasy feelings in your marriage. Look for that healthy balance. Have some "you" time as often as possible and work on your own personal goals. You're spouse won't be able to help but be curious as to what you are doing. This keeps the interest alive.

CHAPTER 9

how to earn interest

Ask any successfully married couple what keeps their relationship alive, and they'll tell you, "Interest." It's as simple as that!

No, I'm not referring to your savings account; I'm talking about fascination sparked by a bit of curiosity. This is the motivator to getting that first date. Something you did or said in your dating days sent out strong "interest" signals to your significant other, which left him/her wanting to get to know you better.

If you played your cards right, you sent out enough strong interest signals to alert the attention of the United States National Security. This of course led to date number two and three, and eventually the exciting idea to share the same last name! Yes, "interest" deserves much credit for bringing the two of you together, because without it you might still be a "table for one" at Larry's Steak and Grill on all-you-can-eat Tuesday night.

According to a study performed by Jeanette and Robert Lauer, authors of *The Quest for Intimacy*, of the 351 married couples that were studied, the marriages that survived were characterized by spouses seeing each other often and viewing each other as best friends. They enjoyed spending time together, agreed on life goals, and noted that they found their spouses more interesting over time.

So how do you earn interest? It's very simple. A wise person once said, "If you want to be interesting, become interested." How profound. Notice the transitive verb "become." This implies that you must "act" in order to get desired results. Isn't that what our parents always told us? "If you want something bad enough, then do something about it!"

They were right, as parents usually are. The more interest you show in your spouse, the more interest your spouse will show in you. You need to give in order to get. That's how we learn who our spouses really are and what they are about. As soon as we lose interest, we are saying we no longer care. No longer caring can eventually lead to finding someone else who cares. It really can be dangerous to our relationships when we no longer take the time to be with our spouse.

This is what many married couples seem to miss most—that exciting feeling when you know someone is watching and wondering about you (someone you admire, of course), when you feel as though you are a book waiting to be unfolded and you know someone is interested in reading your story. One of the best things about being married is that you no longer have to be out on the hunt. You caught what you wanted and now you can enjoy the meal. Remember those days when the person who dropped you off at your doorstep ended up being a different person than the one who picked you up? If only you'd known that ahead of time you would have rather spent the evening playing cards with your grandmother and her friends. We all are nodding our heads. Yet on the contrary, as soon as we found our "other half" the most uneventful date we'd ever encounter didn't seem uneventful at all because we were "getting to know" that person. That's what made sitting in a car for three hours more exciting than spending a week at Magic Mountain.

Now apply this concept to the "date." If it worked so well then, it will work even better now. Think about it—when you were strangers you had so many unanswered questions, the main one being, "Is this person eventually going to be worth investing my time into?"

Often when we unfold a person's pages we start to get information we don't want to know. Sometimes the story we were so fascinated with takes a sharp turn and we lose interest in the ending. Sometimes we regret becoming a main character in a story we had little control over writing. That's just a part of life and we know that ours goes on.

We do, however, have control over our story and our spouse's. In fact, consider you and your spouse co-authors of the story of your life. When you think about your life as a book it changes things, doesn't it? You want to be a part of a story you have control over. Now pick your choice of story: romance, comedy, adventure…you choose (try to avoid a thriller). Isn't this fun? The best part is, you already know your spouse inside and out and therefore you know this story has a great main character. Gone are the days of gaining interest only to lose interest.

So, what do you do if you feel as though your story needs help with a climax? This is where the dates come into play. Every date that you plan is another page to your story. It's new territory to explore. Yes, you may have always known that your wife likes Italian food, but did you know that she's never enjoyed it on top of the roof?

What a fun conversation you'll start as you gaze down at the view below and spy on your neighbors without their knowledge. You may even drop a breadstick or watch a meatball splat onto the driveway, but the point is your wife will enjoy that dinner more than she would have at the kitchen table. The next morning as you pull out of the driveway and you drive over that meatball, you'll smile as you recall the night before.

You see, the best way to gain the interest of another is to put yourself in an "unexpected" situation or environment. Change things up a bit. Dates are a perfect way to do this! When you make the night unpredictable you spark up new ideas and conversations. Your spouse realizes that there is much more to you and the relationship. There are more doors to open, more topics to explore, and more of you to figure out. Thus, your story together becomes more interesting and the two of you will look forward to writing more pages in your book.

One thing I don't understand is when married couples say, "Yeah, but we've reached a point where we know everything there is to know about each other." I say, impossible! There will always be new things to learn about each other. The day you stop learning is really the day you stop communicating.

After an evening of presenting this subject to a group of women, one of them approached me with some insight. She said that she had been married for 11 years and on the evening of their most recent celebrated anniversary she learned that her husband had no idea that she had changed her favorite color three years prior. "I'll never forget the look on his face," she said. "It was as if he finally realized he didn't know me as well as he thought he did. We laughed about it all night and decided we were going to do better at getting to know each other."

I love that story because it's a classic example of the point I made earlier; you never know everything about your spouse. Once you realize this you'll never run out of things to talk about.

People often change their interests as often as they change lanes on the freeway. For example, you may have loved gardening the first five years of your marriage. If you've looked out your front window for the past few years and noticed that you no longer can see where the flower beds meet the grass, then clearly your interest in gardening has weakened. Chances are you'll still speak of it as if it is one of your great interests and you'll feel a bit awkward when you notice your guests giving you a confused look as they leave your home.

It's a good idea to re-evaluate your interests every six months. Sit down and ask yourself what new things you'd like to explore or interesting places you'd like to visit. Share with your spouse so you both can be aware of each other's changes. If you ever feel like you don't know your spouse as well as you used to, it's probably because you don't.

The goal of this chapter is to help you understand the importance of striving for an "interesting" relationship. To be successful at this you must be aware of the three Danger Zones that can lead to an unhappy and uninteresting relationship. They are:

Remember Yesterday

This is when you feel as though someone has taken over your spouse's body and you want the "old" person back. This shows that you are not willing to accept change and adapt to it. This will cause contention and barriers between the two of you. Your spouse will lose your trust and it could damage his/her self-confidence. If you love your spouse you need to appreciate him for who he becomes. He may have been more adventurous when the two of you were dating, but who said there is anything wrong with a quiet day of fishing on the lake?

You'll find there were many characteristics that drew you to him that still are very much a part of him. Take the opportunity to learn what drew him to fishing. Maybe it has nothing to do with even catching a fish! Look for the positive things and build from there.

I do want to caution you that if your spouse's interests have become violent, illegal, or self-destructive you will want to seek professional help for the both of you. You do not need to accept behaviors that are toxic and destructive to the relationship. If there is no harm in the interests your spouse chooses then you must learn to be accepting and appreciative of your differences. Differences can actually bring two people closer together.

Not Another Day

You have entered this zone when you convince yourself that you know everything there is to know about your spouse. You lose motivation in keeping the passion alive. Yes, you may still go out on dates, but your conversation is dryer than the Sahara Desert. You find yourself finishing each other's sentences. It may have been cute when you were younger, but now it's become annoying. You'd like to have more to talk about but it's difficult to bite your tongue when you really want to say, "I've heard that story a million times."

This zone is a sign of pure laziness and bad habits. If your spouse wants to tell her story about her worst prom ever and you've heard it ten times too many, let her. Ask her questions about it. Ask her what she'd do differently if she could go back. Make an old conversation new again. There are always new things to discover if you know the right questions to ask. Also, make your dates more creative. Live a little more on the edge and as if your last day on this earth were tomorrow. What questions would you want to ask your spouse if today were your last day together? There is no excuse for settling into this zone.

Two Peas in a Split Pod

This involves trying to force similar interests upon yourself to gain approval of your spouse. This is dishonest; not only do you cheat your spouse but you cheat yourself! It's okay to dabble in your spouse's interests to see if they are something you'd enjoy as well. It only becomes unhealthy when you forget about yourself and your own identity. If your interests are drastically different, I recommend that you try to dabble. Husbands, it means a lot to your wife when you ask her to show you how she scrapbooks the family photos so well! In fact, if you made a date out of it she'd be blown away. More points for you, and chances are you may actually have a good time! Wives, think of how thrilled your husband will be when you ask him to teach you how the game of football works. Make a date of that, too! You could either go to the park and try out what you've learned or plan to watch the big game—just you and him and a pizza!

Whatever that interest is that your spouse loves and you'll never understand why, take that as an opportunity to get to know your spouse better. Get on his/her level and find out who he/she really is. This shows true love, respect, and unselfishness. Your spouse will appreciate you and in return show more interest in you and your likes. You may know what your spouse's interests are, but do you understand why?

In this changing world around us we can't help but change. Change is what makes our relationships so interesting! Without it there wouldn't be anything new happening in our lives. Your job as an equal in your relationship is to look for change in your spouse and embrace it. When you show a devoted interest in every talent, hobby, desire, passion or goal that your spouse tosses on the table, you are telling your spouse that he/she is important to you. The favor will be returned tenfold. Life will become more interesting!

Note: A fun activity idea for a date night is to prepare a list of 20 questions that you've never asked your spouse before. Have him/her do the same. The idea is to have fun with this. Avoid serious/confrontational questions. An example might be, "If you could change places for a day with anyone in the world, who would you choose and why?" or "If you were told that you had to change your name, what name would you pick for yourself?" These ridiculous questions will lead to interesting conversations which will boost your relationship. Have fun!

CHAPTER 10

icing on the cake

As a lover of Disney movies I can't help but notice the similarities that precede the endings of the favorite fairy tales. Snow White, Princess Aurora, Cinderella, Ariel, Belle, and the others all have something in common—that famous kiss! You know exactly what I'm talking about. If not, you have a date with Blockbuster* this weekend as you clearly have some catching up to do!

Husbands, you may be a little in the dark on this topic. Let me help you out. To most women a kiss means more than just physical touch. It's also an emotional and spiritual connection. If done correctly, it can trigger several other emotions and lead to a grand finale at the end of the night. The best kisses often show no mercy to the grandest fireworks display on Independence Day! To have a great date is a piece of cake, but to top it off with the correct kiss puts the icing on that piece of cake.

Many couples are forgetting the important role that the kiss plays at the end of a date. As they pull into the driveway they are already thinking about the sweet union of head meeting pillow for beautiful solace. What joy lifts their weary eyes when they enter the bedroom at quarter past eleven to be welcomed by the irresistible sight of a lonely mattress longing for the company of heavy sleepers. In fact, it's possible at this point to forgo any dental hygiene as the thought of squeezing a toothpaste tube does not compare to the thought of crashing under the blankets. Though very disgusting, it is most likely happening this very minute somewhere in the world.

You can help prevent this too-common tragedy by slowing it down a bit before heading into the house. After turning off the engine, why not just sit there for a minute and unwind in the car while gazing into the eyes of your lovely other half. Even just saying, "Tonight was fun" or "Thanks for the great time" can be the perfect gateway to the end-of-the-night kiss. I'm telling you that the end-of-the-night kiss is very serious business!

Many wives are nodding their heads right now while circling this page with a bright yellow highlighter. Some wisdom I offer to them is that it's not always your husband who needs to take the lead here. Many men enjoy being surprised by their wives with an unexpected "move" that sends the two of you off into orbit. Remember, it takes one person to make the move, but two people to create the magic!

Making the "kiss" happen before the enchantment of the date is interrupted by crying children, beckoning sleep, or the nightly news is critical to the whole purpose of dating your spouse. It's crucial to take some time before entering your house to make that vital move. The problem with waiting until you're inside your home is that you take the risk of unexpected interruptions and distractions that await you.

People seem to relate entering their home to crossing that bridge from the date (fantasy) back into routine (reality). I recommend the time frame between turning off the car and opening the front door. In fact, the ideal spot for the good-night kiss is always on the doorstep. Before unlocking the door take your wife's hand and sum up your thoughts on the evening. Then look into her eyes, put your arms around her and let nature's forces take it from there. There's something about the nosy neighbors possibly catching a glimpse of your marital bliss through a crack in their blinds that adds to the excitement of that moment, not to mention the breeze and scents of the evening air and the glittery spectacle of stars above. If you are more private I do recommend the car.

Remember that you can't force the kiss. If you're spouse isn't in the mood you'll need to respect that. If your date has been a success thus far, chances are good that she'll be hoping for that kiss. Never rush the moment. You may have a babysitter waiting to collect payment and go home. An extra 15 minutes should not make a difference. This time that transitions you from enchanted evening to reality should be eased back into. Susan Page mentions the importance of this topic when she says,

> "Lovers operate in real time. The usual day-to-day rush simply fades away for them, and they set their own rhythms. The world may be flying past them, but they can't be hurried. Couples who thrive for many years together occasionally find themselves in the little oasis of real time. It may be on a weekend getaway or a long vacation. It might be triggered by a discussion or an emotional event, either happy or sad. The two of them are completely present with each other. They hold each other; they look at each other; maybe they talk or take a long, slow walk. They become unaware of time. It has no control over them; everything happens naturally."

If you truly are engaged in the date and enjoying the company of your spouse time will have no control over you. Everything will happen naturally, nothing will feel forced or hurried. And that is exactly how the "magical kiss" occurs. When you and your spouse seem to be the only ones who exist on the planet you have succeeded at this chapter. Just like with eating a good slice of cake, indulge down to the last crumb!

CHAPTER 11

butter what?

When asked the question, "When was the last time your husband gave you butterflies?" most women can't remember. "Butterflies only happen when you're young," they reply. "The longer you've been married the less they occur. It just means that you're getting older or you've been married too long."

I find this response amusing. I have known couples to be married 20+ years and who still get butterflies. I've also known couples who have been married for five years and have no clue what butterflies are. Let me give a definition, according to Wikipedia:

"Butterflies in the stomach is a medical condition characterized by the physical sensation of a 'fluttery' (hence butterflies) feeling in the stomach. Some believe that this is caused by the release of epinephrine, or adrenaline, when one is nervous, pulling blood away from the stomach and sending it to the muscles. This in turn causes the stomach to temporarily shut down, possibly the reason for loss of appetite when one is 'love sick.' Butterflies in the stomach is most often experienced prior to important events, when stress is induced."

Ah yes, your wedding day, the moment you became engaged, possibly even the first date. Do you remember now?

Ask yourself, "How can I give my spouse butterflies?" and if you have no clue, well . . . try asking your spouse. Wives, your husband will be more than honest with you when you ask him what gave him butterflies in the beginning and what will work now. In return you can do the same for him.

It's important to remember that not everyone gets butterflies the same way. If you get weak in the knees when your wife tickles your neck and you lose your breath when she creeps up from behind, that doesn't mean it will work for her. Chances are you will give her a heart attack if you jump at her from nowhere or she may fall asleep if you tickle her neck.

A recommendation I offer is good old time apart. Absence does make the heart grow fonder. I don't mean getting separated for a while—simply just a week or even a day away will do. Plan an exciting weekend excursion of "girls only" or "guys only." Visit a friend or family member who lives a great distance away. Something about trying to enjoy a sunset or hearing your favorite song play in a small café, miles away from the person you truly love, does wonders on any relationship.

When your spouse sees you get off that plane and your eyes meet for the first time in weeks, you'll revisit all of those feelings you had when you were younger. When you come home from your time apart, make your spouse your top priority. Sweep her off her feet and kiss her tenderly. These are the moments that release adrenaline. Never refer to your excursion as "time apart" in an already troubled relationship. That term can spark up negative emotions. Also, the excursion is not to be used as a means to make the other jealous or hurt. Those are selfish and childish behaviors that will interfere with successfully dating your spouse.

Another idea you can try if time apart is not an option is a little danger and adventure. Try an activity that is bound to release adrenaline. There is nothing that will get your heart pumping and blood racing more than being in the face of danger with the person you love. This could be your last moment together, right? Remember to keep it legal and do not put yourself in a situation that imposes obvious danger, such as having a picnic on train tracks. Try bungee jumping, roller coasters, or if you are brave enough, skydiving. Imagine what is would feel like to be falling thousands of feet while kissing the person you love in mid-air. That should release some butterflies and definitely rejuvenate the magic in your relationship.

Susan Page touches on this subject well when she says,

> *"Couples who thrive are enthusiastic about each other. And they maintain this enthusiasm over many years of their relationship. A woman who is seventy-nine and has been married for fifty-six years to a man who is eighty-three told me, 'I still brighten up when he walks into the room. When he has been away playing bridge all afternoon, I feel excited about kissing him when he comes home and about getting a report on his game.'"*

As you can see, age does not limit these feelings of excitement. The longer you've been married to someone the more you should discover what you love about her. What is it you miss about her when she is away? What was it like the first time you fell in love or laid eyes on her? How can you recreate that experience or get those feelings back? The answer lies in what you are not doing already. Obviously what you are doing has not been working. Take the ideas mentioned above to heart. Make some changes in the way you think about your spouse. Look for what you value and enjoy about her. Look for opportunities to miss her even if it is just from a long day at work.

CHAPTER 12

congratulations!

You are now ready to put what you have learned into practice! Remember, if you're not having fun while doing so, you may need to revisit some chapters in this book. Old habits can be tough to break and what these chapters have recommended may be a whole new adjustment for you and your spouse. The great thing about these practices are that they are fun, easy to do, and are designed to bring you and your spouse closer together. Effort will always be essential to making your spouse feel important. When you find the joy and passion in "treating" your spouse, it will begin to feel effortless over time. As soon as it starts to feel like "work" you need to re-evaluate your motives.

Dating your spouse has no end. Isn't that exciting? The more you strive to make your spouse feel like king or queen for a day the more your spouse will return the favor. Your spouse will begin to reflect the results of your dating. Husbands, when you make your wife feel special, attractive, fun to be around and youthful, she will begin to become all of those things as she will believe that's who she is. Wives, when you show appreciation towards your husband and you go the extra mile in making him feel important, handsome, fun to be with, and the only man you want to spend your life with, he will become that man.

As spouses, we play a big role in the development of each other's self-confidence, self-esteem and self-worth. An entire personality can be destroyed and a marriage ripped apart over the course of just months. It's important that husbands and wives take this subject seriously and learn to build each other up through the simple concepts of dating. It's critical that the older we get the younger we feel. As the years pass, our attitudes towards each other and our relationships should become more positive and our lives should feel more meaningful.

I wish you the best of luck on your dating adventures and I challenge you to start out each day with the intention to notice one positive thing about your spouse and to share that with him/her before going to bed. Forget about trying to "fix" your spouse's flaws. Instead, focus your attention on aspects and characteristics that you enjoy most. After all, those are the things that attracted you to your spouse from the beginning. If you focus on them they will soon become strengths and they will slowly overpower any weaknesses that have interfered with your ability to love your spouse. Make this your motivation.

I encourage couples throughout the world to make dating your spouse a priority! You will soon learn why this is such an important concept and how it can strengthen any relationship. The more couples that apply these principles to their relationship and truly understand them, the fewer divorces and broken families we will see throughout the world. It is my goal to start this new movement and to help the world understand the value of a strong relationship. When we are at peace within our marriage the effects can be astounding! We will raise happier children, become better employees, and overall find the joy in life. Live each day as if it could be the last that you spend with your husband or wife. No regrets. Best wishes to you and your spouse!

CHAPTER 13

50+ best date ideas ever!

This chapter is devoted to offering you some of the best date experiences you may ever have! In fact, this chapter is also a great resource for date planning for teens and singles. I recommend that when planning these ideas, you adjust them to your own personalities and lifestyles. You'll find that when planning these dates, your own ideas will begin to spring forth and you'll create some very unforgettable memories. In fact, if you'd like to share your own creative ideas or just share the experiences you have had from reading this book, please utilize the contact information listed in the back of the book. I'd love to hear from you.

As humans we sometimes become very serious in our many roles and responsibilities in life. It's important to be able to let loose and have some fun. As soon as you're willing to forget about what "others might think" and become more open-minded, you and your spouse are bound to have a great time. When you are able to switch from work mode into "be a kid again" mode, you're on your way to experience some unforgettable memories. Becoming "like a kid" does not necessarily mean you need to act like one. It simply means that you are able to enjoy yourself, not worry, have fun, laugh again, feel silly or excited, and express yourself positively without feeling embarrassed. Bring out the inner child in you and your spouse and feel young again.

Most of these dates can be enjoyed as a double date or in a group setting. Group dates are very healthy for any marriage and are a great way to make life more interesting! I recommend that if you are big on group dating, you start a group "date club." Choose couples that you enjoy spending time with most and reserve a date night once a month for a group date with those friends. Rotate with each couple so that you are not always planning the dates; this way you will be introduced to new ideas and experiences.

Another alternative if you don't have very many friends is to pick one couple (keep in mind they need not be married) and ask them to invite a set of their close friends to be a part of your group date. This is a great way to meet new people and start your own circle or "date club."

Though group dating is fun and highly recommended, it's important that you reserve some alone time for you and your spouse after any date. It's never a good idea to plan all your dates with groups or to let unexpected guests tag along on a date meant for just you and your spouse.

If you are reading this book on your own, you may not want to let your spouse get a hold of this chapter as many of the dates are surprises. If your spouse wants to read the book with you decide how you will approach this chapter. I suggest the person who is the least creative be the spouse assigned to this chapter! Keep in mind that these dates are designed to inspire creativity and thought. Taking your spouse to the opera, basketball games, or a fancy restaurant has all been done. If you're ready for something new, then this chapter is just for you!

Bold, Risky, and Adventurous!

#1 Amazing Race

(This date is best to do as a group date.) Make a list of unique items located throughout the city, such as a take-home menu from a local restaurant, a grocery sack from a specific grocery store, a perfume sample from the mall, a jarful of sand—be as creative as you'd like. All couples meet at a specific location and have one hour to gather the items on the list and meet back at the location.

This city scavenger hunt is a blast and great for those who love competition. You will laugh as you and your spouse try to beat the other couples while racing around town trying to gather your items and beat the clock. You may even run into the other couples at your locations and plot a strategy to slow them down.

When the time is up whichever couple has the most items wins! If couples arrive a minute late they are disqualified. You will laugh as you share your stories and experiences over dinner. For those who like a prize, beforehand agree that the losing couples buy the winners dinner or dessert. It just makes the date that much more fun!

#2 Fear Factor

Decide ahead of time what the winning prize will be. The couple with the lowest point total provides free babysitting, washes your car, makes you dinner, etc.

Set up a series of up to five events to take place that evening. Couples are each their own team. If one spouse decides to sit out during an event the other spouse can still participate and represent the team. Points are awarded to each individual after each event; thus if both spouses participate the more points they will accumulate for their team. The winner of each event receives five points, second-place winner receives four points and so on. All events should be timed. It's always fun to videotape a date such as this. Some examples of events could be:

- Contestants put on embarrassing clothes or opposite gender clothes and head to the store to purchase a pack of gum and head back with the receipt (timed).

- Fun with worms! Make shavings from a block of bitter chocolate and take about four cans of bitter cocoa and dump on a large tray. Bury at least 50 sour gummy worms underneath the bitter cocoa soil. Tie hands behind back and dig through soil with mouth to locate worms. Time this event. Person with most worms wins!

- Line up shot glasses filled with spicy hot sauce. See who can drink the most hot sauce within 30 seconds.

At the end of the night, add up points, proclaim the winners and celebrate!

#3 Scare Affair

Have you and your spouse make a list of things that terrify you, such as karaoke, sky diving, swimming in the ocean, or anything that you have avoided like the plague. Carefully select one item each from your list (this works great if you select the same item) that you would like to finally experience.

Discuss with each other beforehand why you are terrified and why it's important that you overcome your fears. Once you are both in agreement begin planning your date. Make a small contract that each of you sign to avoid backing out at the last minute. List a consequence if contract is broken, such as washing and detailing the car, or hour-long massages for a week. Also list a reward for those who face their fear, such as dinner at a favorite restaurant, or a weekend out of town. The purpose of this date is to take your relationship to new levels of growth.

As you both face your fears and complete your experiences you will discover a new respect and attraction for each other. You will also develop a new level of confidence. Chances are that you might actually enjoy your experience and decide to do it again.

This date is ideal for M&M couples who feel bored and at a standstill. This date is certain to throw some excitement back into your marriage!

Dates For Budgeters

#4 Creative Coupons

So you have absolutely no money to spend. How can you still treat your spouse and have a great time yourself? It's simple—homemade coupons. Make a coupon book for your spouse with all the services you are willing to offer and then surprise her with the book the day of your date night. Tell her that she may only use four coupons that night so to choose wisely.

Some examples might be "Coupon good for..." a 30-minute massage, a love-song serenade, playing any game of your choice, making spaghetti and meatballs, making homemade pizza, reading entries from your high school diary, one slow dance, painting your toenails, etc.

When making the coupons, select ideas that you normally would not do, such as watching chick-flicks, making dinner from scratch or anything that is out of the ordinary for you. The purpose of these coupons is to let her have control of the evening and feel like a queen for a night. She will appreciate your willingness to enjoy activities with her that you normally would not. In return you will enjoy the way she reacts to your kindness, and trust me, you won't be a bit sorry!

#5 Olympic Games

You can do this date at home, in a park, a field or up in the mountains. You're going to be setting up a series of Olympic events for you and your spouse. This date works great with groups as couples can compete together. Make a gold, silver, and bronze medal out of construction paper or purchase plastic ones from your local party store.

Set up different events that complement each of your strengths. Some easy ideas are basketball, swimming races (in a lake or pool), leg wrestling matches, arm wrestling, thumb wars, bike riding, running, rope climbing, archery, winter sports, pie-eating contest, relay races, obstacle courses, etc. You may even need to travel to different locations to compete in your events.

When the events are over, award the winner of the most events the proper medal. You may even consider awarding a medal after each event. Not only is this date a lot of fun, you also burn a lot of calories!

#6 Dinner with a View

Don't worry, this date doesn't require a fancy restaurant or hotel. All you need is a picnic basket, blanket, maybe a candle and a car.

Locate an area nearby that has a great view of the city lights. If you don't live in the city pick a different view such as a lake or the mountains. Wash your car and pack an easy dinner, such as sandwiches, a bucket of chicken, or get drive-through. Grab a freshly laundered blanket and a candle in a jar.

Hide the food in the trunk along with the blanket. Close to sunset, tell your wife you are taking her with you to run some errands. You may even want to run a couple of places so she has no idea. She'll be surprised when you take a detour and drive to a beautiful lookout point.

Set up the blanket on the hood of the car and light your candle. Pull out the dinner and enjoy the beautiful view and the cool night breeze. She'll be so surprised that she won't care how little money you spent!

#7 Free Golf

If you can round up some Frisbees, dart guns, foam/plastic sports balls, or a toy bow and arrow you are almost set! All you need is something to hit your targets with. Go to a park area where there is plenty of space and trees. Prepare your targets ahead of time by taking paper plates and taping or tying them to the trees. Eight targets should be enough. For fun you can write words on them like "Yeah Right!" or "Too Hard" or paste funny pictures on them.

The rules are just like golf. Always go for the hole in one! It's fun to keep score unless of course you are too competitive. Later you can enjoy lunch on the grass. If the area you choose is rather secluded, set up a picnic behind the tree at the last target. How surprised your spouse will be to discover a delicious lunch waiting to be enjoyed!

#8 Dream Date

Okay, if you and your spouse love to dream and are goal-oriented, then you're going to love this date!

Locate some nice areas where there is new development within a 50-mile radius of your home. Plan to visit at least four large and beautiful model homes. You are going to pretend that you are in the market for a new home. After all, eventually you will be looking and when the time comes you'll have an idea of what you want. The idea for this date is to dream big. Whether it's a home with a view, lake-front property, or just a bit bigger and newer than what you have, the sky is the limit.

Plan to tour at least three model homes that evening. Call ahead of time to schedule an appointment or just drop in. Usually when you don't have an appointment the sales agent will let you tour the house on your own, or you can request this. Walk through the house and point out what you like and don't like. Take a pen and note pad with you to take notes. Talk as though you are going to purchase the home. Say things like, "Would the bed look okay here?" and "Where can we put the office?" By doing this, the dream becomes a reality while you are in the home. They say that those who dream big achieve big!

Realize that this date should in no way stir up depressed or envious feelings. You should have fun and not walk away wishing you had what you can't afford. Start talking about what you can do to achieve your goals. Make a five-year plan. You may not be able to afford the homes you toured, but you can take ideas and inspiration from them to motivate yourselves and decide what you want in a home you can afford.

Go to dinner afterward and share your dreams together. Write your plan and your goals down before the night is over. Post them on the fridge or by your bathroom mirror. If you see them often, you'll strive to achieve them. This date is very motivational and inspiring!

Dates for Bonding and Connecting

#9 Trust is a Must

This date is great for building trust and having confidence in one another. It will also teach you to be open-minded. You are about to be at the sole mercy of your spouse.

The rules to this date are that your spouse has complete control over your look for the evening. You will both be getting the other ready for the date! Yes, your husband will style your hair, pick out your clothes and put on your makeup. You cannot offer any hints or suggestions. He will pick out your jewelry even down to the shoes, purse and jacket.

In return, you will style his hair and pick out what he wears and even how he smells. Keep in mind that you want to make each other look as nice as possible. This is not an opportunity to tease your spouse. You are not allowed to say anything bad about how you look.

Once you are both ready, with a smile on your face go out to dinner and a movie or whatever you have planned for the evening. Make sure to take pictures so you can always remember this night. You may be surprised at what your spouse is capable of. Have fun!

#10 Blast into the Past

Sometimes living in the past isn't such a bad thing! It's time to recharge your time machine and take a trip back to yesterday.

If possible plan your date in the area where you two met and dated. If you met at college, plan to eat at your old hang-out spot after attending a college basketball or football game. Take a stroll around the campus before you head off to see a movie at the theater where you had your first date together. If that is not possible, rent the first movie you saw together. If you went ice skating on your first date, then go ice skating! You don't need to re-create your first date, just pull your favorite moments from when you were dating and incorporate them into your date.

For authenticity purposes, try to wear a sweater or outfit you wore when you were dating. If it doesn't fit anymore find a hat, jewelry or shoes that you may have worn. Dress young again! Put together a CD of the songs that were popular when you first met and play them in the car. Roll down the windows and enjoy the fresh air from your past. As you revisit old places and take a trip down memory lane, you will enjoy connecting and rebuilding your friendship. This date is sure to make you feel young again!

#11 Wishful Thinking

Turn those thoughts and wishes into your reality! This is fun, easy, inexpensive, and a great way to bond.

Collect or purchase a variety of magazines on topics such as fitness, real estate, beauty, home and garden, etc. You will need two large poster boards, scissors, glue, tape, and markers. Purchase or borrow the DVD entitled *The Secret* (or any other motivational video or tape).

After dinner, watch this DVD together (it is also available to watch online). Then make a list of the areas you would like to improve in your life, such as health, habits, finances, spirituality, etc. Begin looking through the magazines for photos that best illustrate these goals. Cut and paste them on your poster board until you are out of space.

When you are finished, take turns presenting your posters to each other. Be considerate and uplift one another. Talk about how you can help each other achieve your goals.

When you are finished, display them in an area of your home where you will see them often. Decide that a year from that date you will revisit your poster and see what you both have accomplished. This is a fun way to connect and uplift each other!

#12 Intimate Interview

Make a list of 20 questions you have never asked your spouse before. Have him do the same. (You may need to give your spouse a week's notice to come up with questions.)

An example of a question might be "If you could have any job in the world other than the one you already have, what would it be?" or "What is a dream you always had as a child that you never sought after and why?" or "If you could have been born and raised anywhere else in the world other than where you were, where would you choose and why?"

Take your spouse somewhere for dinner in a cozy and quiet environment with few distractions. This date is great for dinner conversation when couples feel they have little to talk about. This date is also great for connecting as you and your spouse will explore new topics together.

You may learn some new things that surprise you. This should spark a very interesting conversation. You will feel important as your spouse expresses a desire to know more about you and you do the same for her.

Note: Make sure your questions do not bring up unpleasant issues or any contention as that is not the purpose of this date. You want to have a good time and feel closer.

Dates Celebrity Style!

#13 Fancy Fantasy

This date is perfect for those who fantasize about living the celebrity lifestyle. You may not have tickets to an award show or invitations to an elaborate ball, but there is still a chance for you to walk the red carpet. (This is fun for a group date or party.)

Ahead of time you will need to arrange to rent or borrow an expensive car or limo. If that is not possible, arrange to have someone be your driver for the night. Make sure the car that you use has been freshly cleaned inside and out. Have in the backseat a bottle of sparkling pear juice or whatever you prefer to drink along with champagne glasses. Make sure to have a toast before you start off your evening.

Dress to impress in your most elegant clothing. Remember this is celebrity style, so think Hollywood, *GQ*, and the Oscars. Get your hair done in a salon and get yourself some sparkly accessories. You can purchase cheap costume jewelry and imitation diamonds from the mall. From a distance who will know? Husbands, get some designer cologne samples from the mall so you can smell like a million bucks without having to spend it. Impress your spouse like you never have before.

If you do this date as a party or with a group, pick a dinner location where you will be able to roll out the red carpet (purchase red fabric from your local fabric store). Possibly rent a dining room from a hotel, network amongst your friends to borrow a condo or summer home, or just pick any restaurant that will accommodate you. Send out invitations to all who are invited or just to your spouse if it's the two of you only. Hire family and friends to roll out the red carpet upon your arrival and to stand off to the side snapping pictures (resembling the paparazzi). Afterward you can develop them and have some good laughs. Just for kicks, hire a family member or friend to walk up to you and ask for autographs. This will really confuse the public as they try to determine who you are.

Fill your wallet full of bills, even if they are all $1 bills. You will be expected to tip a good amount that night, so be prepared. Enjoy your luxurious evening with your celebrity entourage. You'll have fun as you notice all eyes on you. You'll find that you get better service and treatment everywhere you go. You may even get asked for an autograph. Have fun with it. After all, it is just a fantasy!

#14 Make a Statement Using Your Spouse!

Have you ever imagined your spouse with a different look? Maybe your husband doesn't get excited about fashion or your wife is stuck in a fashion nightmare. Maybe neither of you have purchased new clothing in the last 12 months. No matter what your reason, this date is a great excuse to get some new clothes!

No need to panic! First of all, this is just a date, so if you are not satisfied with the results remember that tomorrow you can go back to being the old you. Second of all, you don't need to spend a lot to get a lot.

Get your spouse's measurements and sizes and decide on a limit, such as $50 each, $75 each or whatever you can afford. It may be fun to pick a celebrity ahead of time that you would like your spouse to resemble. Each of you will go to the mall prior to your date and pick out an outfit that you think your spouse would look fabulous in. You may want to consider shoes if your spouse doesn't own very many. Make sure you don't go over your limit and if possible have some money left over. It will be fun to see who can create the best look without spending the most. You may even want to try a thrift store for gently used clothing. This will allow you to stretch your dollar that way and if your spouse hates it, you aren't out very much cash. Save receipts just in case.

Avoid shopping with your spouse as it's likely to create arguments and defeat the purpose of the date. If your budget allows it, take your spouse to the salon to get his hair styled the way you'd like it. Avoid haircuts and hair coloring unless your spouse consents. That way if he hates the look it's not permanent.

When its time for the date to begin, present each other with the outfits you have chosen. The rules to this date are that you have to agree to wear the look your spouse has chosen for you even if you dislike it. Realize that you may feel ugly or out of place, but your spouse will be eyeing you up and down all night. That's the goal!

Once the look is complete go out to dinner or to a movie, just make sure you show your look off to the world! Remember to take pictures as you may never get your spouse to wear your look again. Also, make sure you have fun and laugh with this. Who knows? You may actually love your new look!

#15 Shopping Spree! (Don't worry, you won't be broke!)

This indoor date is great on a rainy or cold-weather day. Instead of letting the bad weather get you down, take some of that money you have saved for a "rainy day" and put it to use!

Buy a mall gift certificate to your spouse's favorite mall. The only rule is you can't leave the mall until all the money has been spent. Let her decide on where to eat and what to buy. Have fun!

#16 Your Debut Single

Sunny and Cher, Jessica and Nick, Tim and Faith, and all the other musically talented married couples in show biz have had one thing in common—they've made sweet music together! Whether or not you sing, can carry a tune or know what an F sharp is, this date will blow you away!

You and your spouse are going to write a song about your life together. It can be funny, romantic, or whatever describes your relationship best. Spend an evening writing the lyrics to your song and later try to hum a tune that will work with your lyrics.

Contact a local recording studio in your area and call around to get the best price. Let them know what you are doing so they realize this is just for fun. Otherwise they may want to charge you for mixing and fine tuning. You may be looking at about $50-$100 per hour, depending on the studio. Let the producer know in advance that you don't want to exceed a certain price. For sake of time, the producer may select a beat for you as well as the instrument sounds.

If your tune is simple the producer often can play it for you on a guitar or keyboard. If you don't have a tune you can sing along to a beat, do a rap, or sing acapella. When you are happy with the tune and sounds, you will go into the studio and record your voices. Some studios will record your lyrics first and add the instruments later. You will likely mess up more than once so be prepared to laugh and have fun. You may want to capture some of your laughter on the actual recording.

When you are finished make some copies for your friends so everyone can enjoy your new hit single! Play the song often in your car when you are out together; it will create a chuckle and bring back fond memories. Use it as an icebreaker when you are on double dates. It will always stir up a conversation. Also, when you encounter rocky moments in your marriage, just play this song and it will be hard to remain upset with each other.

#17 Dinner and a Date

This isn't just any dinner! Hire a chef or someone you know in the culinary arts program to come and cook for you personally. It may even be your best friend's sister who happens to be a fantastic cook!

Ask the chef to prepare a menu a week in advance of his/her specialty dinner. Include appetizers, drinks, and a dessert. Present the menu to your spouse and let her choose what she'd like for dinner.

Give your order to the chef and allow him to purchase the groceries and cook the dinner in your home. Ask your chef to set your table in accordance to the dinner he is preparing. Allow him access to your dishes. Don't forget the tablecloth, candle and roses. Leave the door unlocked so that your chef can come over and cook while you're at the movie.

Take your spouse to a movie or play and tell her that dinner will be later. When it's time to go eat tell your spouse that you want to eat dinner at home. Be prepared for her to look at you strangely and try to talk you into going to her favorite restaurant.

Act as though you want to save money or you're not in the mood to wait in a line. As you walk into the house with your spouse, she'll see the nicely set table and flowers and wonder who has been there. Have the chef come out (dressed as a chef) and introduce him. Your chef should also act as your private waiter. Have the chef bring the bill at the end of dinner along with any receipts and make sure you tip well!

You and your spouse will enjoy this fancy dinner in the privacy of your own home without having to cook. What a way to eat like a celebrity!

Dates for Unwinding and De-stressing

#18 Moonlight Massage!

This date requires no work, just an appointment!

Ahead of time you will need to contact a spa and book an appointment for the both of you. Now of course you could book an appointment at the spa and enjoy the already created relaxing atmosphere...or you could be a bit more creative and hire a masseuse or two to come to your home.

Make sure the house is clean. Choose an area in the backyard such as your deck or patio. Bring out a stereo and play soft music. Light a few candles or tiki torches and line them around the patio. There is nothing more relaxing than feeling the cool night breeze run across your back while getting a massage with scented oils. You'll want to make sure the weather will be warm enough.

Let your spouse know ahead of time so she can prepare. She may want to shower first and possibly shave her legs to get the best effect from the massage. Enjoy a light dinner such as soup and a salad, and when the masseuse arrives, you'll be ready to go.

#19 Hanging Out

It's been a long week and you are just too tired to go out. This is a great alternative to the typical date. You are going to need a hammock, drinks, and relaxing music. If you are too tired to leave your house, just tie the hammock in your backyard right at sunset.

Preferably drive to a secluded location where you can tie your hammock between two trees. Lay there with your spouse, sipping drinks, listening to music and just relaxing. Being away from distractions out in nature at sunset or under the stars is always golden.

#20 Late-Night Laughs

Laughing always feels good!

Get online and order/rent your favorite comedian acts. Go with a comedian that suits your style. You can check out ratings and what fans say to help you decide. You are going to bring comedy into your home! If you can't decide on a comedian, then rent your top three favorite comedy movies of all time. You and your spouse may have a different sense of humor, which is why you need to let him be a part of this decision.

Buy a bunch of treats and snacks and spread them out all over a blanket on the floor. Get fun items such as gummy worms, Pop Rocks, jerky, etc. Get in your PJs and lie on the floor with your spouse. Laugh and munch the night away. This is an easy way to have fun without having to entertain each other.

#21 Savor the Sunrise

Sunsets can often be a bit overrated. It's time to celebrate the dawn!

Arrange for someone you know to set up a small table and two chairs overlooking a small waterfall, pond, lake, stream, ocean or any type of body of water. Provide her with some fresh flowers and dishes. You'll want to either prepare breakfast ahead of time and secretly pack it in the car or have your helper make breakfast and set it up. Some good breakfast ideas are strudels, French toast, strawberries and cream, and of course orange juice!

Wake your spouse up early while it's still a little dark and tell her to change into something comfortable. Drive her to the location and surprise her with breakfast. Eat and watch the sunrise together. You may want some music playing as well or have someone serenade you with singing or a violin piece.

This date is very romantic but also peaceful and relaxing with the sounds and view of the sun sparkling over the water.

Dates Unusual Yet Fun!

#22 American Idol

Yes, it is a singing competition, just a step up from karaoke. For group dates or parties, locate or borrow a karaoke machine that provides the song lyrics. They are very reasonably priced if you decide to purchase one for yourself. Invite over your friends and recruit yourself three judges. Have your judges dress, talk, act, and critique like Randy, Paula and Simon.

Before the competition starts have everyone drop $1 in a box. The winner will collect the cash prize. Have the contestants draw their song choices randomly from a hat. This makes it more fun! Also, have a duet round where couples sing together. After each performance everyone in the room will silently rate it on a scale from 1 to 5 and drop their ratings in a box in the back of the room. At the end of the night all ratings will be tallied up and the top three will be announced. Those three will then have another round of competition and the room will silently vote on who they like best. Make sure your judges rate each performance and give feedback to the contestants.

Award the American Idol with a medal, trophy, certificate or just the cash prize. You may want to videotape this event for blackmail purposes later!

#23 Strangers in Love

This date requires a good imagination and acting skills. You and your spouse are going to pretend you have never met. The purpose of this date is to rekindle old feelings and of course to have fun!

Pick a crowded place where you two will meet, such as a dance, café, club, carnival, theme park, etc. Select your location and time. Make sure you avoid each other as much as possible that day until the time of your date. Get ready in separate places and take separate cars. One of you should arrive 15-20 minutes prior to the other. Now remember, since you are strangers you can make up new names for yourself, new interests and hobbies, and of course make up anything you want! This makes it feel as though you really are getting to know each other for the first time. You won't be able to help but laugh; try to contain yourself.

You can either pretend you have been set up on a blind date or one of you walk over to the other and offer a cheesy pick-up line. Those observing will really think you are strangers. They may even look at you judgingly as you both will be wearing wedding rings. Make sure you ask the usual first date questions such as "Where are you from?" or "What do you do for a living?"

Give whatever answers you please while trying to maintain a serious face expression. Try to really believe what you are saying as well as your spouse. You'll begin to notice others around you eavesdropping, especially if your new identity is a bit outrageous. This should be motivation to make your conversation more interesting. You may even want to hire a friend to follow the two of you around with a video camera, just to make things more interesting. The public will assume you are on a televised blind date. If anything, it will be fun to watch your date later and applaud your acting skills.

You'll have fun getting to know each other in the most unusual way. It may be a bit difficult to snap out of it when you get home. You may want to stay in character until the next day. This date is absolutely hilarious!

#24 Tales of a Talk Show

This date works best as a group and is a lot of fun!

First, you will need to find someone who is willing to be your talk show host. For fun have him dress in a suit and tie and sport a fake mustache. As you call your friends and invite them, ask them if they want to be audience members or guests on the show. If they want to be guests, ask them to pick one issue with their spouse that they would like to discuss on the talk show. Of course the issue should be something minor such as leaving the toilet seat up, clothes on the floor, or a soda-pop addiction, etc. The title of the show will be "Out-of-Control Spouses." For those who want to be guests, ask them to make a five-minute video clip about their out-of-control spouse. Of course ask them to exaggerate the issue and make it fun.

Set up your family room with audience chairs and a stage area where the host and guests will sit (near the TV). At the beginning of the show have your host remind the audience to applaud at the beginning, when the guests come out, and at the end of the show. You may want to film the show and give everyone who attended a copy. It's also a fun idea to play the cheesy music at the beginning, when the guests come out, and at the end of the show.

Give your host cue cards with brief information about each guest. Have the first spouse come out and introduce herself and explain why she is on the show. Then play the video clip of her spouse displaying his bad habits. Have the talk show host ask her deep questions about the issue, such as, "And how does it make you feel when he puts the empty milk carton back in the fridge?" Allow audience members to stand and comment. (They will have fun with this.) Have the host walk around with a microphone.

Then of course bring the husband out and have everyone in the audience "boo" him. Allow him to argue his point and have the talk show host and audience members convince him to change his ways.

At the end of the show, have the host quickly introduce a product on the show such as lemonade or a pack of gum and announce to the audience, "And . . . you're all getting one!" The audience will cheer loudly as packs of gum or cans of lemonade are tossed into the air.

Have the host thank his guests for being on the show followed by a cheesy closing line such as, "Remember, if it's important to you, it's important to me."

This is a hilarious date activity and your friends will talk about it for months to come.

#25 Surprise Getaway

This date definitely is a surprise!

Arrange ahead of time for two people to be your kidnappers and for someone to pay a ransom. Your spouse may be alarmed at first but will eventually catch on. If your spouse works, call her employer ahead of time and arrange for your spouse to be granted time off that afternoon without her knowing it. Ask her employer to play along. Have her boss call a meeting that includes your spouse and others. Ten minutes into the meeting have your kidnappers come in and ask for your spouse. Ask everyone in the room to look alarmed when this happens.

When your spouse leaves the room, have your friendly kidnappers explain that she is being kidnapped by the orders of someone else. Have the kidnappers tie a blindfold around her eyes so she cannot see where she is taken. You may want everyone in the room to applaud and laugh at this point so she realizes her life is not in danger. Have them wish her luck on her kidnapped adventure.

Have your kidnappers take her to a location where you will have a nice table and two chairs set up. You may want to borrow someone's backyard or pick a hidden spot outdoors she will not recognize by scent or sound. Have one of the kidnappers sit by her in the backseat to make sure she doesn't peek.

When they arrive at the location, have them ask her for her husband's phone number. The kidnappers will then call you from the car and say that your wife has been kidnapped and they need a pretty good ransom in order to let her go.

Have them start by asking for money and then have them say

to your wife, "He says you guys don't have that much cash in the bank. Is that true?" Get her in the middle of it. The kidnappers will then go back and forth with you on different ransom ideas. Finally you will suggest a delicious family recipe, such as her sister's lasagna or her mother's pork roast. The kidnappers will then discuss it for a bit and say, "Okay, if this is as good as you make it sound, we're ready to make a deal."

Your kidnappers will then give away the location. Allow them to let her take off her blindfold but not to let her see the table and chairs. Have them say to you, "You have 15 minutes to be here with your sister's lasagna or your wife will disappear for good. Oh…and bring your sister, too!"

Have them put your wife on the phone and say, "Don't worry, I'll be there soon. Do you think your sister will mind?" Of course you will have arranged with her sister ahead of time to do this.

Arrive at the location and tell the kidnappers you called her sister and she said she will hurry and make the lasagna but it may take a half hour as she has to boil the noodles. Have the kidnappers get anxious and say that isn't good enough—if she doesn't come in five minutes the deal is off.

Just then her sister will come into the backyard with a nice batch of hot lasagna and everyone will applaud. Your wife will then realize the joke is over as you take the lasagna over to the table and chairs that await. Everyone will then leave as the two of you enjoy a nice lunch/dinner together outdoors. It will be fun to hear what your wife has to say!

Afterward take her out to a movie and grab dessert. She'll have so much fun while the rest of the world is still at work.

Note: If your wife does not work, you can still do this. Arrange for a friend of hers to come over and visit at the time of the kidnapping. Explain to her your plan and ask her to stay and babysit so your wife can leave the house.

#26 Murder Mystery Dinner

You can do this date with a group or with just the two of you. This date is terribly fun and keeps the conversation flowing all night!

Find a good friend or family member who will play your butler as well as the storyteller. Make up a short murder story with about eight characters, including one who gets murdered. In the story list five or more locations, such as the garden, the library, the garage, etc. You will also mention objects throughout the story, such as a hammer, a bottle of pills, a baseball bat, etc.

To make your story interesting, one of your characters might be a professional baseball player or a pharmacist. Have the characters tie in together, such as they were attending a charity banquet or filming a movie. Hint toward possible motives throughout your story, such as "the producer's wife was seen leaving in a taxi with the star of the movie at two in the morning." In the end have one of the characters die and the body is found in a shallow grave.

You will write the story but will have your butler/storyteller decide who the murderer was, where the victim was murdered, what the motive was, and with what weapon. This way you can play the game as well. Tell him to be creative with it. Print off copies of the story along with a list of locations, weapons, names of characters, and a blank space for the motive.

Set up a long dinner table in your home designed for a feast. Place a copy of the story by each place setting along with a pen. This way your guests can take notes and have all the information they need. If you invite a group, plan your dinner ahead of time and ask each couple to prepare a specific food item.

Your butler is also going to make clues and present a different one at the time of each course. Have him make the clues difficult just for fun. He will present each clue on a silver platter.

At the beginning of dinner your butler will ring a bell or dim the lights to get everyone's attention. He will then say that you all have all been gathered here tonight for a special reason. He will then tell the story of a murder that recently happened in the area and ask for everyone's help to solve the mystery so the town can rest. After he reads the story (in a British accent), he will announce that the mystery must be solved by the end of dinner. There will be a prize for the winner. The guests must decide on a murderer, motive, location and weapon.

As the butler brings out the appetizers he will also bring out a silver tray with the first clue. Ask someone to read it or pass it around. He will continue to bring a clue until after dessert has been served. Watch as everyone has fun discussing the mystery while enjoying the delicious dinner. When the dinner is over ask everyone to put their pens down. The butler will then announce that the mystery has just been solved and will read the results. Whoever has the most guesses right will win the prize!

Note: Ask everyone to bring $1 and the winner can collect the cash at the end of the evening, or use it to pay your butler for his services.

Dates with the 3 E's: Explore, Educate, Experiment

#27 Discovery Date

All you need is a full tank of gas and a map!

Locate a map of your entire state. This is easy to do if you have the internet. Choose a city or town that you have never been to, or even better, never heard of. You may even want to list the different towns on slips of paper and choose one from a hat. Pull up the city or town on the internet to see what you can learn about it. Learn what there is to do there.

Prepare for your small road trip! Pack a cooler of snacks and treats and bring your favorite CDs. Don't forget your camera! This is a lot of fun when you are unfamiliar with the roads and territory. You'll enjoy new scenery and experiences. You might even get lost! Be prepared.

When you arrive begin exploring and experimenting. Try out a new and interesting restaurant there. Visit a museum, local theater, or just sightsee. Drive through the neighborhoods and look for beautiful and interesting homes. Go to a local park and talk to the people there. Find out what there is to do for fun in the area. Make new friends and new memories. You might enjoy it so much that you'll visit again!

You can repeat this date many times as there are always new places to discover! Try out new restaurants, walk new trails, and enjoy new scenery!

#28 Culture Night

This date opens up doors to new experiences!

Make a list of as many different cultures as you can think of, such as Chinese, Latin American, Polynesian, Southern, African, Native American, Italian, etc. Cut up into slips of paper and draw from a hat. If you were to select Southern, for example, your date would be centered on this culture. You might want to try out a southern food restaurant or learn to cook southern recipes from the internet. You may want to rent a travel video that takes you on a tour through the southern states. Practice speaking in a southern accent and learn the mannerisms of that culture. Enjoy southern music such as Cajun or bluegrass. Find someone who is from the south and ask her to give you ideas or share experiences.

If you chose Polynesian, you may want to learn some island dances. Look in the phone book to see if there are any Polynesian dance classes offered. You may want to invite someone over to cook Polynesian food for you and teach you some phrases in the native language. For Latin American, you could learn to dance the salsa and dress in colorful clothing!

For every culture you should be able to find something in the phonebook, at the library, video store, or on the internet to complement your date. The goal is to learn and experience something new and to also develop an appreciation for diversity.

#29 Dance Fever

If you have two left feet, it doesn't matter. It wouldn't be a new experience if you were already good at it!

Contact a local dance studio in the area. Call and make an appointment for private dance lessons or sign up for a class. Choose a style of dance that is easy for beginners. You might want to ask the instructor for suggestions.

Spend your evening learning the dance and technique. Afterward go out for dinner. Your feet will probably be a bit sore and your body a little tired when you get home. Take a warm bubble bath and give each other a nice foot rub.

Make an effort to practice what you learned throughout the week. By the next weekend gather up the courage to go and test your new abilities. Enjoy dinner and afterwards visit a local club where you can show off your new dance moves. You'll have a lot of fun even if you are off-beat and the center of attention!

#30 Foreign Flicks

Who doesn't enjoy a good movie on a comfortable couch? This date is great for rainy or cold weather.

Take a trip to the video rental store and make a mental note to avoid the "New Releases" section. Your job is to hang out in the foreign film aisle until you find a movie that interests you. The movie you select will either have subtitles or voice over.

Either way, be prepared. At first you might be a bit bothered by this but as the movie goes on you'll soon forget the annoyance and enjoy the story line.

There a lot of good foreign films that you probably have never heard of. It's always a good idea to ask the video store clerk for suggestions or check out options online before you head out.

This is a great way to change up the typical "rent a movie" date. Make a large bowl of popcorn and roll out some blankets. You're in for a treat!

#31 Score Some Skills

This is great for discovering, learning and entertainment all in one.

Look through the classified adds in the local newspaper for classes offered. School districts often offer their facilities for classes taught to the public. Select something you've always wanted to learn or else know nothing about. These classes are often very affordable, but you must call ahead of time to sign up.

Have fun as you learn the art of pottery, painting, singing, cooking or sewing. Remember that it's always good to be open-minded and give everything a fair shot! You never know, maybe your husband will discover that he's actually good at knitting quilts!

#32 Historical Happenings

Do you know the history behind your city?

Many people live within a few miles of a museum and don't even know it. This is a great opportunity to learn more about the city where you live and the story behind it. Look in the phone book or online for the museums closest to where you live. Call to schedule a tour. You don't have to travel far to learn something new!

If you don't mind traveling far, locate the nearest ghost town or "haunted" landmark. This makes for a fun scare and nice getaway! Share your experience with friends and family.

#33 Field Trip

Everyone longs to be young again. You'll feel like you're back in elementary school!

Select a place that you would enjoy touring, such as a candy factory, bakery, car company, toy factory, famous cave, or even a film studio. Call ahead of time to find out when tours are given. Give your spouse a signed permission slip allowing her to attend the field trip!

Pack lunches in a paper bag or buy lunch boxes. Make peanut butter and jelly sandwiches and don't forget your bag of chips! For the full field trip effect, take a bus to your destination (if the bus line runs there). Have fun as you learn something new together!

Dates for the Romantics

#34 Would You in the Woods?

This cozy date is ideal for getting away and getting close. After a nice dinner, head to the woods or nearby forest and make sure to pack a jacket! (The idea is to end your date before sundown.) You will need matches, lighter fluid, an ice-cream maker, a generator, and the ingredients for your ice cream. If you don't have an ice cream maker, buy ice cream from the store as well as toppings for a sundae. Don't forget the ice cream dishes and spoons!

Hook up your generator and get your ice cream going while you and your spouse stroll hand in hand through the woods. Go on a small hike to search for your firewood. Don't wander too far and get lost. When you get back light a small fire and enjoy your ice cream in the privacy of the trees. You will find that homemade ice cream really hits the spot!

Something about being in the woods can be enchanting yet a little frightening and you may want to scoot a bit closer. By the time you are finished you should begin to feel cold from the ice cream. That's the secret! You will want to cuddle and maybe share a blanket while you enjoy the fire as the sun sets.

What a way to end the night!

#35 Movie with the Stars

After this date you will never want to sit in another stuffy theater again.

Ask your spouse to pick her most favorite chick-flick of all time. Throw a blanket down in the backyard on the grass. Borrow an old sofa or take one from your house and move it to the backyard on the blanket. Toss a bunch of pillows on the sofa and the blanket as well as a comfortable quilt.

If you are able to, set up a projector that faces the back of your house. You will be watching the movie on your house. If needed hang a white sheet on the house for a screen. If you don't have access to a projector, a TV will do just fine. Buy a bunch of your favorite snacks or treats and you are ready to go!

Enjoy the show while you snuggle together under the stars. There's something very romantic about being together outside in the dark. Enjoy!

#36 Dinner on the Lake

Why spend money on a cruise when you can enjoy this idea instead?

Locate, borrow, or rent a small canoe or fishing boat. Be careful with a canoe as they tend to tip over easily. Prepare a meal that you won't need to eat at a table, such as pizza, gourmet subs, grilled sandwiches, or a bucket of chicken.

It's always best if you prepare something homemade. You can make it romantic by bringing along wine glasses and sparkling cider (or your drink of choice). Make a CD of all your favorite love songs and bring along a battery-powered CD player. Be careful not to drop it in the lake!

As you paddle out toward the sunset locate an area of the lake where you can float the boat for a while and enjoy your dinner. Have a toast and enjoy each other's company. Let the music serenade your dinner. You'll enjoy the sound of the waves and the sun dancing on the water as you exchange passionate kisses.

#37 Pillow Talk

You might need to buy yourself a new pair of PJs just for this occasion!

Yes, this could be a group date and you could invite couples over to wear matching pajamas, but the category for this date is titled "Dates for the Romantics." Need I say more?

Begin by draping fabric all around the family room. Choose colors such as black, chocolate brown, red, or pastels. Take white Christmas lights and run them along the ceiling to create the appearance of stars. Put some black sheer fabric over them to create a night sky.

If the weather is warm, open up your windows for a nice breeze. Try to incorporate satin sheets, stuffed animals, and several pillows into the décor. You want the room to look as inviting and comfortable as possible. If you have a fireplace, light a fire. If not, burn scented candles. Make sure you both wear comfortable slippers.

Locate or borrow a fondue set and enjoy fondue for your dinner and dessert. Some great snack ideas are strawberries and whipped cream, bite-sized chocolates, and of course sparkling cider.

Purchase some love dice and have fun! Give each other a back rub. End the date with a romantic comedy. Prepare to spend the night in your family room. Yes, it's okay if you fall asleep during the movie. The best part about this date is that you are already ready for bed!

Theme Dates

#38 1950s Night

Surprise your spouse when he walks through the door with a blast from the past! When he smells the burgers and fries and sees you in your poodle skirt and ponytail he will forget all about his long day at work.

This date is ideal if you have limited time as you can order take out from your favorite fast food spot. For a healthier alternative, make your own burger bar. Set up a buffet of burger fixings and bake your own fries. I like to make my own dipping sauces for this occasion. See the recipes on the next page.

This idea is great if you have bar stools. Decorate the kitchen or wet bar like a 1950s diner (napkin holder, salt and pepper shakers, mustard and ketchup bottle, '50s celebrity photos). Make sure you have your '50s music playing in the background and don't forget the chocolate shakes!

You can download your own mix from the internet and pick your favorites. A great substitute for a jukebox is to print a list of your songs numbered in order of how they appear on the CD or a list of your iPod tunes in alphabetical order. Post it on the wall next to your stereo so requests can easily be made. If you are having a group date, your guests can be their own DJs.

After dinner you might want to swing to a few songs or slow dance to a '50s love ballad in the kitchen. When you're finished don't let him leave the house without his leather jacket. Finish the evening with a double-feature movie at the Drive-In. Surprise him again with a treat basket for the both of you complete with all your favorite snacks.

This date will bring out the "teenager" in both of you and you'll soon forget about the stresses and responsibilities of adult life just for a night!

Fifties Fry Sauce

½ cup of mayonnaise
3 tbsp. ketchup
1 tsp. lemon juice
3 tbsp. pickle relish
1 tbsp. minced onion
Mix together and enjoy! Great on burgers as well.

Sweet & Zesty Southwestern Sauce

½ cup of Miracle Whip
2 ½ tbsp. Smokey Chipotle Tabasco Sauce
2 ½ tbsp. ketchup
1 tbsp. minced onion
A dash of garlic powder
Mix well and serve!

#39 Caribbean Nights

Get ready for an evening of adventure and good food, "Matey!" (This idea is great if you don't have a babysitter and the kids will be present. It is also great for a party with your close friends.)

Make your own "skull and crossbones" napkins by tracing and cutting out from the center of each napkin (or draw with a magic marker). Roll up the napkins and use eye patches to wrap around them (like a rubber band) as napkin holders. Make sure everyone wears their eye patch during dinner. For the table centerpiece, fill a treasure chest or jewelry box full of chocolate gold coins and candy necklaces, bracelets and ring pops (unwrapped).

Set it on a rolled-out treasure map that you can make out of construction paper (don't forget to burn the edges of the map for authenticity). Have the jewels and coins spilling out of the box and across the map. Serve Caribbean food (see the accompanying recipes).

After the feast, watch *The Pirates of the Caribbean*. If you have seen the movie too many times, a fun idea is to have a treasure hunt. The map used as your centerpiece can be the actual map for your family treasure hunt. The clues can be hidden throughout the house and even folded up inside the napkins. The treasure chest should be hidden somewhere in the house and the clues lead to the location.

For a back-up centerpiece, take a fish bowl or glass casserole dish and fill with blue raspberry Jell-o. As the Jell-o starts to set in the fridge, place gummy or Swedish fish in the Jell-o. Top with Cool Whip and place atop a toy pirate ship, boat, mermaids, palm trees or any other theme-related item. You now have a view of the sea on your table that also becomes a part of your dinner! Enjoy!

Jamaican Jerk Chicken
1 pound skinless chicken breasts
1 jalapeño pepper, seeded and diced
3 tbsp. water
2 tbsp. lime juice
2 tbsp. lemon juice
1 tbsp. Dijon style mustard
4 cloves garlic, mined
2 cubes chicken bouillon
½ tsp. ground cumin
¼ tsp. dried thyme

Combine all ingredients except the chicken and pour into a shallow baking dish or sealable plastic bag. Add chicken and turn to coat. Cover and place in refrigerator to marinate in jerk seasoning for between 4 hours to overnight.

Preheat grill. Remove chicken from jerk marinade and pour marinade into a saucepan. Bring to a boil. Place chicken on grill cooking approximately 7 to 10 minutes per side (or until done), basting periodically with remaining jerk marinade.

Caribbean Shake

1 small papaya, peeled, seeded, and coarsely chopped

1 mango, peeled, seeded, and coarsely chopped

1 ripe banana, peeled and coarsely chopped

1 ½ cups whole milk

2 tablespoons sugar

1 cup crushed ice

Combine the fruit in a blender and purée to break everything up. Add the milk, sugar, and ice; blend until thick and frothy.

#40 It's Amoré!

This is sure to be the cheapest and next-best thing to a weekend in Venice! Bring Italy to you. The best part about this night is that it actually feels like a date. Your spouse will be picking you up at the front door just like old times.

Have your spouse rent a nice hotel room ahead of time for the evening or weekend. Let him surprise you as far as the location and if he wants to decorate the room with chocolates and roses, etc. As soon as he picks up the keys, have him get ready at the hotel and you get ready alone in the comfort of your own home. Yes, ladies, you will have it all to yourself!

Turn on your favorite music and sing and dance while you dress up for the night (just like old times). Set a time for the date to begin and have him drive up to the house and ring the doorbell (preferably with a bouquet of flowers). The purpose of this is to create the excitement of going on a date and to set the mood for the evening. Anytime you step away from routine and the norm of your marriage you are bound to have more fun and fall in love again.

If possible, create a CD ahead of time of the songs you and your husband enjoyed during the time you were dating. Have that playing in the car throughout the entire evening. By now it should feel like it did when the two of you were in the butterfly stage.

Go for Italian take-out. Fazoli's is great if you have a tight budget (they have a dollar menu). Take your dinner up to the canyon or to your favorite lookout spot. Even better, if you have the means, enjoy dinner on a small boat or canoe out on the lake at sunset. Bring a portable CD player and play Italian music, such as Andrea Bocelli. If not on a boat, play the music from your car as you eat your dinner on a picnic blanket. Burn a candle while you enjoy your Italian food and get to know each other all over again. Fill two wine glasses with sparkling grape juice and have a toast in the moonlight.

Pack up and go out for Italian ice cream. Enjoy your dessert in a cozy ice cream parlor and afterwards stroll around the block holding hands. Finally, it's time for your man to take you back to his place. End the evening at the hotel. Go for a swim at the pool and later cuddle up to a romantic comedy. Suggested movies that complement the theme: *Only You, Life is Beautiful* (foreign film), and *Chocolat*.

#41 Fixed on Fashion

If you've ever wanted to participate in a fashion show, walk the runway, or pose for a camera, this will be a lot of fun. (This date works best as a group date or party.)

If doing as a group date, send out invitations to your friends with the following information. Everyone is to create a "high fashion" outfit that they will wear that evening. The object is to be creative and invent something that you really would only see on the runway and would not be caught dead wearing in public. For best results, shop a secondhand store or yard sales. The more outrageous the clothing is, the better. There will be a contest as to who the best designer is. Also, announce on the invite that dinner will be potluck. Assign each person a food item to bring.

Wherever you decide to host the date, set up a small runway using either a strand of Christmas lights to outline the stage, a platform, or roll out some fabric or construction paper. Set up chairs around the stage. Get some good runway music with a fast beat and set up by your stage. Also, set up a banquet table for your "fashion feast." The goal is to make it look elaborate while poking fun at the theme. For example, use tiny dessert plates in place of dinner plates, giant peacock feathers in a large vase as your centerpiece, miniature handheld mirrors lined up with the silverware at each place setting.

Have your guests arrive wearing a robe over their clothing to keep it a surprise. When everyone has arrived, begin the fashion show. Give everyone a slip of paper to cast their vote for best design. Have each couple take their turn modeling on the runway, one person at a time. When they are ready to walk, they will take off their robe to reveal their design. Have everyone "ooh" and "aahh."

Assign someone to be at the foot of the stage snapping pictures of each model. Also, you may want to film this for laughs. By the end of the night you can print the photos and hand them out to your guests as they leave. Offer a prize to the winner.

You may want to rent a comedy that goes along with the theme, such as *Zoolander*. Enjoy your dinner and maybe go out in public just for kicks!

Note: If you decided to do this without a group, have a photo shoot instead of a runway. Set up an area in your house with a fan blowing, a fabric backdrop, and some accessories. Have your spouse be your photographer and instruct you on how to pose. Do the same for him. Later you can develop the film and have something to laugh at, or you may be pleasantly surprised. You can also add this idea to the group date and take couple snapshots having each couple strike a pose. Just like Homecoming pictures!

#42 1980s Prom Night

Anyone can do this date. The question is, are you willing?

This date is best done as a group. First you will need to decide where you want to have your 1980s prom. Use your connections to locate an available space—in your basement, a school, a hotel, an empty warehouse, outdoors etc. Next you will need to design a cheesy theme such as "Forever Young" or "Love under the Sea." You will want this theme printed on your invitations and of course on a large banner at your prom. Charge $3 per couple to pay for your refreshments and pictures.

Announce on the invitation that '80s prom attire is a must and there will be a prize for the best outfits. Suggest shopping at second-hand stores. Purchase some cheap decorations such as crepe paper, balloons, and a disco ball. Don't forget the punch and cookies!

Create a collection of '80s music and set up your stereo and speakers. Set up an area with a chair, a rubber tree, and some balloons for pictures. Assign someone to take pictures of each couple. After the party e-mail or print copies and send to your friends.

This will be a night to remember. Enjoy as your friends break out all the old dance moves while sporting forbidden hairstyles. You may want to film it, too. Have fun!

#43 Redneck Ruckus

It's time to celebrate "ugly"!

This group date is a lot of fun. It's cheap and easy to do. You will need to start by creating the appropriate atmosphere. Place an old couch on your front porch or lawn. You might put one in the backyard as well.

For décor, try a hideous welcome mat, wind chimes made of tin cans, car tires, aluminum lawn chairs, paper plates, mismatched mugs with cheesy logos, and don't forget your redneck rock music!

Ask your guests to wear redneck attire such as T-shirts with the sleeves cut off, frayed jeans, mullets, hats with ridiculous sayings, Billy Bob teeth, and to arrive barefoot. Enjoy a BBQ in the backyard with chips and soda. Offer a prize for the best dressed couple. Don't forget to take pictures!

Play games such as arm and leg wrestling, thumb wars, cards, tug-a-war, and wheelbarrow racing. You'll enjoy as the neighbors stare at you looking a bit confused. Remember, "If it ain't hurtin' nobody, ain't nobody got to say nuthin'" or something like that.

Dates for Staying Home

#44 Backyard Golf

Not only is golfing in your backyard more private, it's also free! Locate or borrow a set of golf clubs and balls. Take nine hard plastic cups or jars and place them on their sides throughout the backyard. You are going to set up your own miniature golf course!

Make sure the lawn has been freshly mowed. Set up small ramps, barriers, tunnels and obstacles in front of each hole. Make it as tough or simple as your heart desires. The object, of course, is to hit the ball into the cups. Be as creative as you'd like and don't forget to keep score!

Suggestion: This date is great to do while making homemade ice cream in the backyard. Also, plan to have a picnic on the grass or a BBQ!

#45 Let Fate Plan Your Date

Make a list of unusual places in your house and yard where neither of you spend much time, such as on the counter, in the bathtub, on the front porch, on top of the washer and dryer, on the roof, etc.

Both of you will create your own separate lists for all items without showing them to each other. Cut them up into strips and place in a jar. Next, make a list of games that you can play with two people, such as cards, checkers, or tic-tac-toe (be as creative as you'd like). Cut those up into strips and place in a jar. Make a list with your spouse of movies you'd both like to rent; cut into strips and place in a jar.

Finally make a list of dinners you would like to eat, such as pizza, stir fry, tacos, etc. Cut into strips and place in a jar. Also, make a list of desserts and cut into strips as well.

First, one of you will pick from the dinner jar. Let's say you pick burgers. You can decide to go to the store and buy the patties and grill them at home or go through the drive-through. Either way you will eat them at home. The other will then choose from the location jar. Let's say you pick the kitchen counter. You will do the same for the game and the location where to play the game as well as the movie and dessert.

So your date might end up being something like: Go shopping for buns, cheese, and meat, then come home and fire up the grill. Enjoy burgers on a picnic blanket on the kitchen counter. After dinner, hop into the bathtub and play two rounds of checkers. Later, watch his favorite comedy while enjoying her favorite dessert. And who knows, maybe a little time alone up on the roof!

The purpose of this date is to make staying home feel different for once. If you always eat dinner at the dinner table, how exciting is that? You'll find that spending time in unusual places will spark up unusual topics and you won't be able to avoid laughter. So, you can have your usual dinner, game and movie, yet enjoy them in a most unusual way.

Also, you will avoid any arguing over what movie to rent or what to eat. Once it is chosen from the jar, the decision is made. If your spouse is unhappy just blame it on fate! "Well honey, it's not my fault. I guess this is meant to be." Have fun!

#46 Backyard Campout

So maybe one of you prefers hotel sheets with access to a shower over a flannel sleeping bag under the stars. Now you can have the best of both worlds. Eliminate the dirty elements of camping and keep the beauty of being outdoors.

Set up a tent in the backyard along with lawn chairs, sleeping bags, and all the necessities for a night out in the wilderness. Depending on where you live you may or may not be permitted to have a fire burning in your backyard. If this is not an option, try an outdoor wood-burning stove to give that effect and allow for roasting marshmallows. If anything, you can microwave some s'mores and enjoy them on your lawn.

You'll want to do everything possible to feel as though you are miles away from home. This means turning off cell phones and only entering the house to use the bathroom or in case of emergencies.

If you have a garden or mound of dirt in your backyard, this is great for Dutch oven cooking. You can get some great recipes online. Tell ghost stories or sing songs while you're waiting for the food to cook. Another great dinner idea is fire-roasted hot dogs! Straighten out some metal hangers and use as sticks. For dessert, you've got electricity close by. Perfect for homemade ice cream! What a fun night you'll have. The best part is, no packing up in the morning—you're already home!

#47 The House Hotel

Either the two of you never have a reason to spend the night at a hotel, or you figure, "Why spend $50 when you can just sleep at home?"

Sound familiar? If so, this date is for you. This is the type of date where you will want to surprise your spouse. You will need to prepare everything ahead of time and may need some help with setting up.

You are going to be transforming your home into a hotel.

Borrow or locate some sheer fabric. You will want something that is easy to hang as you will be using it to close off certain sections of your home. An easy way to do this is to tie a rope from one end of the room to the other and drape the fabric over or use clothes pins to hang it. This way you can close off messy or unromantic areas of your home. Also, you want to make it look more like a hotel than a house. Turn your dining area into the hotel restaurant. In fact, you can serve buffet style and have your dinner items pre-cooked and sitting out ready to serve.

You'll want to use a small table and dress up with a tablecloth, fancy dishes and silverware, and some candles in the center. Collect all of the house plants and rubber trees and place them around the dining area to transform the look. If weather permits, you may even want to set up your fancy table outside.

Turn your family room into a ballroom by simply rearranging the furniture and providing enough room for dancing. Also, set up a small area there with drinks and refreshments. Hang your fabric to hide what you don't want visible, such as the TV. Take some white Christmas lights and line the entry way or floor in the ballroom. White lights look very elegant under sheer fabric. Think romantic when creating your atmosphere. Put some plants and trees around the room and light some candles.

Take a couple chairs and place them in the hallway with a vase of flowers in between. You may even want to make small signs labeled "grand ballroom" or "master suite" and hang them above the rooms.

For the master suite, dress your bed in an unfamiliar bedspread and use different sheets. Place chocolates on the pillow and some rose petals. Have faint music playing in the background and light candles around the room. Hang some fabric from the ceiling over the bed to transform the room. Place a vase of fresh flowers on the dresser to freshen up the room. Have a bubble bath ready for the "hot tub" and some sparkling cider and glasses. For fun, get a small fridge and fill it with snacks and drinks. Place a TV in your room for late-night movies.

When your spouse gets home and walks through the door she will surprised to find that she has entered a hotel. Check her in at the lobby and give her a key to the room. This night will be a night to remember and it won't feel like home.

#48 Private Club

If your spouse has two left feet, can't feel a beat and has never been the club type of person, then this date is perfect! Now you can both enjoy going to the club without the fear of embarrassment.

Choose the largest room in your home or use the backyard. Take either colored or white Christmas lights and line the ceiling and dance floor. Get a disco ball, smoke machine, or other flashy light contraptions and strategically place around the room. Program your stereo ahead of time to play your favorite songs in the order that you'd like or select random. You can find these items for very reasonable prices on the internet.

Set up a wet bar in the corner or back of the room for drinks and snacks. Don't forget the little umbrellas, napkins, and straws. You may even want to hire family members or friends to be your bartender and/or DJ.

Set up a platform in the center of the room or locate a large piece of plywood for your dance floor. Set up a karaoke machine and microphone by the stage. You might even want to get a projector and play colorful images on your wall or videos along with your music. Also, hang some sheer fabric behind the stage and shine a lamp behind it. This is fun for silhouette dances!

You are now ready to dance the night away! Dress in your clubbing gear and prepare to burn some calories. Invite your friends over or have it just be the two of you. After all, if no one is watching, you won't have any explaining to do!

#49 Water Works

It's the middle of summer and you're dying to cool down. The thought of spending $20 to not only wear a swimsuit in public but to also share the same pool of water with 1,000 or more other sweaty bodies just does not sound too appealing. It's time to bring the water park to you! (This works great as a group date, party, or if you have the kids.)

Borrow or locate a large basin or kiddie pool. Place in the center of your backyard and fill with water. If you have a swing set or slide, place the pool in front of it. Take a roll of plastic (garbage bags, smooth tarp, or purchase a water slide) and lay it across the lawn in between the sprinklers. Buy a bag of water balloons and water guns from the dollar store and fill them up; set aside in a cooler. Set out lawn chairs, beach balls, umbrellas, towels, and a cooler of cold drinks. Set up a volleyball net or tie a rope between two posts.

Rub yourself and your spouse down with sunscreen or suntan lotion and grab all of your swim gear. When ready for the fun to begin, turn on the sprinklers. Slip and slide across the lawn, slide or swing into the pool, enjoy a water fight or play a round of water balloon volleyball using towels to catch and toss the balloons over the net. Play your favorite upbeat summer songs or beach music as you make a splash with your sweetheart and friends.

Note: If you make this a family date, have the kids play a big role in setting it up. If they are involved from the get-go, they will enjoy themselves endlessly while you and your spouse find a quiet corner in the yard to bathe in the sunlight and sip drinks. Remember, it's always important to find those quiet moments to have one-on-one interaction.

Dates When You Don't Have a Babysitter

#50 Role Reverse

If your kids are going to be a part of your date, you might as well make them useful!

If your kids are old enough, tell them that they get to be the parents for the night. They will get to decide what is for dinner, make it and clean up. If this idea doesn't go over too well, you can say, "We are going to play restaurant!" That should work.

Tell your kids they get to set the table, make the food, and surprise you. Someone should be the hostess, waiter, cook, bus boy, and dishwasher; let them choose.

In return for their services they will be rewarded at the end of the night with ice cream sundaes. Tell them that you and your spouse are going to the movies (really the family room to watch a movie) and to call you when the reservation is ready (or of course if they need help).

Sit back and relax with your spouse as you enjoy some quiet time together. If you are worried, you may want to lay down some laws, such as no using the stove, oven or knives. Use microwave for cooking and the toaster is okay. You may also want to offer some food ideas or place an order ahead of time such as sandwiches or hot dogs (something easy for your kids to make).

Your kids will enjoy themselves so much it won't feel like work at all. You'll enjoy them serving you for a change and cleaning up the kitchen. After the kitchen has been cleaned, play games together and enjoy ice cream sundaes!

#51 Box Car Drive-In

This is the next best thing to taking your kids to the real drive-in! Ahead of time locate a large-sized box for each family member. Tell your kids that they get to make their own box cars and will be driving them to the movies! You'll need construction paper, markers, glue, and scissors. You may want to make the cars in the backyard to avoid a mess.

While everyone is making their cars, rent a movie, order a pizza, or make something simple for dinner that the kids will be able to eat in their box cars. When the cars are finished, let the kids drive them into the family room or the backyard (wherever you'd prefer to watch the movie).

Set up a table with dinner, drinks, and snacks so the kids can get what they need and take it to their cars. They will enjoy sitting in their boxes and watching the movie while you and your spouse sit in the back and snuggle together without interruption!

#52 Gimmie Me a Break!

It's time to break all the rules!

Give your kids permission to actually break the rules! You are going to make a list of "New Rules" on a poster board. Remind your kids that these new rules are just for that night and that when the date is over all rules will go back to normal.

Some ideas for new rules could be eat dessert before dinner, eat dinner on the floor, stay up an hour later, play loud music, etc. Post your new rules on the wall where everyone can see. You're kids will enjoy seeing a lighter side to mom and dad as they are given permission to break the rules.

You'll have fun eating dinner as a family on the floor and enjoying a handful of gummy worms or cookies before eating the main course. Afterwards crank up the music and allow the kids to dance on the couch and be silly.

It sounds like chaos, but if your kids are usually pretty good at minding all of your rules they shouldn't go overboard with this date. Enjoy!

#53 Indoor Camp-Out

This date is perfect to do when the weather is bad.

Begin by setting up a tent in your family room. Have the kids help. Let them bring the sleeping bags and a stuffed animal inside the tent. Have your kids get in their PJs as well as mom and dad.

Enjoy a simple dinner, such as hot dogs or pizza. If the weather outside is cold, make some hot chocolate. For dessert, make smores in the microwave. All you need are graham crackers, chocolate bars, and marshmallows.

Tell ghost stories in the tent with a flashlight. Let the kids rent their favorite movie and let them watch it from the tent. Your kids will have so much fun being in the tent that they won't notice mom and dad sneaking off for some alone time during the movie!

#54 Juice Bar

Who knew that drinks, a bar, and dancing could be perfect for kids?

Set up a bar either indoors or out. Buy different choices of juice, such as apple, orange, grape, mango and some sparkling soda. Get a bowl of fresh fruit and some snacks. Purchase some fun straws, plastic cups, and little umbrellas.

Let the kids dress up with sunglasses, flowers in their hair, hats or whatever clothing they want to dance in. Play music and let the kids dance and mix their own drinks. Mom and Dad may want to be bartenders and mix the drinks for the kids. It might be fun to have a drink menu. Include smoothies, frozen slush, and even chocolate shakes!

Provide the kids with silly string, glow necklaces, and whistles. Let them have their fun while Mom and Dad get their groove on as well. The kids will enjoy watching Mom and Dad shake the room!

#55 Snow Blast

Who said snow had to put a damper on things? (This date obviously only works in the winter.) Dress the kids warm in their snowsuits and mittens. As a family build an igloo or snow castle in the backyard. Make a spot where you can build a fire (if this is permitted where you live). When the igloo is finished roast marshmallows over the fire and sip hot chocolate in the igloo. Enjoy lunch or an early dinner in your igloo while dad tells ghost stories.

The kids will be so worn out by the end of the day that they will be ready for bed earlier than usual. This will allow you and your spouse plenty of extra alone time!

BIBLIOGRAPHY

Alle, Gage John ed. *Webster's Dictionary.* (Ottenheimer Publishers, Inc., Baltimore, Maryland, 1990.)

Chapman, Gary. *The Five Love Languages.* (Northfield Publishing, Chicago, Illinois, 1995).

DeFrain, John and Olson, David H. *Marriage and the Family: Diversity and Strengths, Third Edition.* (Mayfield Publishing, Mountain View, California, 2000.)

Harley, Willard F. Jr. *His Needs Her Needs for Parents.* (Fleming H. Revell, Grand Rapids, Michigan, 2003.)

Landrum, Jim and Nancy. *How to Stay Married & Love It!* (River Publishing, Anaheim, California, 2002).

Linamen, Karen Scalf. *Pillow Talk* (Fleming H. Revell, Grand Rapids, Michigan, 1996.)

National Institute of Mental Health, "Depression" (Accessed 9 March 2007), www.nimh.nih.gov/healthinformation/depressionmenu.cfm

PAIR Project, "Results-Abstracts-PAIR Project Writings on Courtship" (Accessed 7 Feb 2003), www.utexas.edu/research/pair/ourresearch/abstracts.html#F

Page, Susan. *Now That I'm Married, Why Isn't Everything Perfect?* (Little, Brown and Company, Toronto, Canada, 1994.)

Satir, Virginia. *The New PeopleMaking.* (Science and Behavior Books, Inc., Mountain View California, 1988).

Sewell, Marcia. *Pilgrims of Plymouth.* (MacMillan, New York, New York, 1986.)

Wikipedia, "Butterflies in the Stomach" (Accessed 14 March 2007.) www.en.wikipedia.org/wiki/Butterflies_in_the_stomach

ABOUT THE AUTHOR

Born and raised in Sandy, Utah, Lindsey has been writing since the age of eight. In 2003 she received a Bachelor of Integrated Studies degree from Weber State University. Her degree emphases are in Communication, Family Studies and Social Work.

As a former employment counselor for the state of Utah, Lindsey has worked as a certified instructor for the Department of Workforce Services, teaching assertive communication and job retention skills. Lindsey has also designed curriculum for and instructed self management and relationship courses. Her "How to Date Your Spouse" class was the inspiration behind this book.

In the late summer of 1999, Lindsey met her husband Manuel who was also studying at Weber State University. They were married on December 1, 2000. Manuel who is a German citizen is also a former semi-professional soccer player from Hof, Germany. The story of how they officially met and the events leading up to their marriage are so unbelievable that Lindsey wrote a biography about it. Eventually she'd like to publish it. They have one beautiful son together Gabe, and a daughter on the way.

Lindsey and her husband are both entrepreneurs with big dreams and ideas. Lindsey firmly believes that the impossible can be possible.

Feel free to visit **www.howtodateyourspouse.com** to contact Lindsey and to learn more about other upcoming projects.